Donatella Mazzoleni

Palaces of Naples

Photography
Mark E. Smith

Historical Research by
Ugo Carughi

Donatella Mazzoleni
Palaces of Naples

Photography
Mark E. Smith

Historical research by
Ugo Carughi

Layout
Stefano Grandi

Translated from the Italian by
Marguerite Shore

First Edition
December 1999

Arsenale Editrice srl
San Polo 1789
I - 30125 Venice, Italy
First published in the United States of America in 2000 by Rizzoli International Publications, Inc.
300 Park Avenue South
New York, NY 10010

ISBN 0-8478-2216-8
LC 99-076241
Printed and bound in Italy

Photographic reference
Archivio fotografico Scala, Florence: p. 16-17, 21
Donatella Mazzoleni, Naples, p. 11, 134, 150-151
Luciano Pedicini/Archivio dell'Arte, Naples: 18-19, 22, 27, 32-33, 85, 86-87, 210-211
Marsilio Editori, Venice: p. 13
Sprintendenza per I Beni Ambientali e Architettonici, Naples and region: 64-65, 66, 90-91, 128-129, 163, 166, 212, 219, 250, 311

Table of Contents

7 Palaces and the City: images, materials, landscapes of aristocratic life in Naples
- *Naples*
- *Vocation and Destinies*
- *Rules*
- *"Palatium"*
- *Backdrops*
- *Giants*
- *Urban blocks and individual elements*

35 Palaces and Villas
Ugo Carughi

36 *Typology*

38 *Palazzo Penne, Palazzo Diomede Carafa, and Palazzo Petrucci*
44 *Palazzo Cuomo*
52 *Palazzo Venezia*
60 *Palazzo Filomarino*
68 *Palazzo Marigliano*
78 *Palazzo Casamassima*
84 *Palazzo Cellammare*
94 *Palazzo Sangro di Sansevero and the Sansevero Chapel*
116 *Palazzo Corigliano*
124 *Palazzo Maddaloni*
132 *Palazzo Reale*
150 *Palazzo Donn'Anna*
162 *Palazzo Sanfelice and Palazzo dello Spagnolo*
168 *Palazzo Serra di Cassano*
176 *Palazzo Reale di Capodimonte (Royal Palace at Capodimonte)*
192 *Reggia di Portici (Royal Palace at Portici)*
210 *Albergo dei Poveri (Poorhouse)*
220 *Villa Campolieto*
236 *Palazzo Casacalenda*
246 *Palazzo d'Angri*
258 *Villa Floridiana*
266 *Villa Acton Pignatelli*
278 *Palazzo Ruffo della Scaletta*
288 *The Corner Palace of the Galleria Umberto I*
298 *Grand Eden Hotel*
306 *Castello Aselmeyer and Villa Ebe*

317 Selected bibliography
319 Addresses of palaces
320 Index of names and places

Palaces and the city: images, materials, landscapes of aristocratic life in Naples

This book on the palaces and villas of Naples is part of a series dedicated to monumental dwellings in the historic cities of Italy. It is not intended as a book of architectural history, although, naturally, it can be seen as a source for historical background information and bibliographical references. Rather, it is meant to tell a story, more through images than words, from the inside as well as the outside, about the present-day life of historic residences that still preserve the forms of a privileged existence. With these dwellings, great sacrifices sometimes have been made in order to maintain continuity with a distant past. At other times, however, tools of modern restoration have made it possible to uncover qualities that had been lost. In some instances, a desire for absolute conservation has removed the dwellings definitively from life and frozen them forever into museums. Only in rare cases have changes over time been judiciously accepted and the buildings' functions and forms transformed accordingly.

We will speak of the *forms*, but also of the *meaning*, that the presence of these dwellings assumes in the city today. This book would not have been possible without the cooperation and collaboration of many institutions, public and private, to whom much of this architectural and artistic patrimony is now entrusted, as well as the help of private individuals who allowed us to explore the interior landscapes of their homes. We have chosen to document only what still survives today, and thus we decided not to mix direct experiences and memories, photographic documentation of the present and iconographic representations of the past. Therefore, the photographic documentation of the buildings and their interiors, rigorously current, shows only a portion of what a traditional strictly historical approach to these buildings would have presented. On the other hand, we have included images that would have been rejected by traditional historical research, which is oriented exclusively toward a restoration if not a celebration of the past and is suspicious of present-day transformations.

Many palaces, renowned throughout history, have been sold or simply abandoned over time and destroyed. Other extremely significant dwellings still exist but have not been properly documented because they have been profoundly

preceding page
Naples, from Castel Sant'Elmo. To the left, the fabric of Graeco-Roman Neapolis is clearly visible, particularly a section of the east-west *decumanus inferior*, now called "Spaccanapoli."

The body of the city: volcanic tufa, which makes up the soil and subsoil, is also used as a building material.

altered by neglect and building speculation, as in the case of the magnificent Palazzo Spinelli di Tarsia. Others have been subjected to perennial restoration work that has enclosed them for years on end in scaffolding—the fate of the oldest dwellings, the Palazzo Penne and the extremely beautiful Palazzo Carafa di Maddaloni. Many historically famous interiors can no longer be seen today, having been either destroyed or made unrecognizable on account of structural and interior design transformations, changing social conditions that made it impossible to care for them, and lack of economic resources for their costly maintenance. Some fascinating and well-known interiors, while still in existence and easily located, are not accessible. Their furnishings have been dismantled, or they are now reserved exclusively for their current owners' private use (e.g., the great hall of the Palazzo Maddaloni, the princely apartment of the Palazzo d'Avalos with its neoclassical reception hall, and Benedetto Croce's private study in the Palazzo Filomarino). And there are numerous prestigious private apartments, known to jealously house exclusive collections of art and antiques, which we cannot mention, having failed to receive their owners' consent. In compensation, we have gained access to other interiors, completely transformed by their current use, which reveal unexpected qualities and have taken on an absolutely unexpected and new charm. (The *Wunderkammer*, made from the Sbrizioli-De Felice study, comes to mind, where the original theater of the Palazzo Donn'Anna has been gradually transformed since the 1960s.) In any case, this book attempts to document both the patrimony that is available today for historical and artistic observation, acting as a witness to a cultural past, and the dwellings that have been intelligently sensitive to change and the creative transformations of life.

This photographic documentation is obviously also an invitation: to journey physically through these spaces in Naples; to see these works "in the flesh" and at close range; to hear the resonance of their rooms; to touch their surfaces; to come into contact with their architectural and artistic identities, within the multifaceted and mutable urban identity of a grand, ancient city that is evolving rapidly. The invitation is extended to the traveler: to people who want to know the spaces of the world, their architecture and art objects, to people who seek experiences with a sense of humility, curiosity, and openness. The invitation is extended to those who feel more comfortable spending time carefully admiring the work and things of others than satisfying some desire to own them for themselves; to those who have no need to plunder souvenirs but prefer the wealth of memories and even forgetfulness. In other words, this invitation is extended to those who know how to enter the houses of others, in a complex city, with awareness, respect, and a desire to understand.

Nevertheless, a book with this approach does run certain risks. The aristocratic and precious dwelling is observed and analyzed under contemporary conditions—no longer seen in terms of historical, diachronic relationships, but instead immersed in a system of synchronic relationships with the urban context. As a result, a certain "suspension of judgment" becomes necessary and, in any case, is exercised. But with a city like contemporary Naples, if this suspension of judgment is excessive and the subject is addressed too acritically, the result, all too easily, can take a perverse slant.

Palaces and luxurious villas, here as elsewhere in Europe, constitute the remains of a representational system that originated in the bourgeois society of the late Middle Ages and the Renaissance, developed dramatically in *ancien régime* society of the seventeenth and eighteenth centuries, and then evolved consistently throughout the nineteenth century, alongside the rise to power of the bourgeoisie. Finally, for all practical purposes, it vanished at the threshold of the twentieth century, surviving, possibly, as pure kitsch fetishes, sold on the antiquarian and tourist markets, or, with great effort, transformed—in name or in fact—into museum pieces.

Any discussion of the palaces and villas of Naples, past and present, must take into consideration what this city has become in recent years: a multiethnic and multicultural crossroads of Europe and the Mediterranean, a theater where west and east, north and south meet. Naples is an observatory and crucible of the great, inexorable migratory disturbances that are completely annulling the historic question of "class struggle," both in Europe and worldwide, and the old "southern question" in Italy, through the superimposition of a considerably broader and more complex issue of planetary globalization. Naples today is a city where many different cultures have their roots, a place where traditions are becoming translated and are changing. It is a city where new cultural languages are developing and being put together, emerging amid the interstices of both buildings and cultures. It is a city where spoken languages include Neapolitan and Italian, but also Polish and Croatian, Sinhalese, Filippino, Arabic, international English, Maghrib French, and the tribal languages of Black Africa.

Aristocratic dwellings unmistakably and obviously refer to a past concept of absolute power, to a way of life based on social differences and on an inequitable distribution of wealth. And so these dwellings also refer to a subtext, the ancient and brutal exercise of force for the maintenance of privilege. In reference to *this* city, then, the exposition of the traditional apparatus of representation—exclusive enjoyment and public ostentation—risks appearing, depending on one's viewpoint, too strong, that is, provocative and exhibitionist, or too weak, an obsolete, anachronistic celebration of social forms that have moved toward inexorable extinction. An acritical, conventional and aestheticizing view of this material would be, in effect, simply reactionary, stimulating either a nostalgia for ancient inequalities and lost privileges or a renewed and more dangerous arrogance. It would also, of course, be historically incorrect. Be that as it may, it is only through the definition of a critical viewpoint—which has occurred in the compilation of this book—that it becomes evident how, within the social context and in terms of current economic conditions, this residential patrimony is tragically being besieged by two opposing temptations that lie in wait: the museum and the market. It also becomes obvious how difficult it is, outside these two paths, to find spaces of natural survival.

It will become more necessary than ever to exercise a comparative vision, focusing on the subject, but neither ignoring nor forgetting the context of the complex relationships in which it is immersed. In this city, perhaps more than elsewhere, aristocratic palaces and villas represent the forms of an elitist way of life. The grandeur of that life is appreciated, but, at the same time, the price that has been paid for it, the other side of the coin, must be exposed and understood. This book does not aim to speak of privileged dwellings by confining their meaning and fate to the past or turning them into rhetorical celebrations of it. It presents these palaces in the present of which they are a part, as living testimony to *one of the many* languages of habitation that interweave within the great multicultural melting pot of Naples today.

Naples

A phenomenon of rare topological consistency, Naples grew, accumulating twenty-five hundred years of history without ever losing its emphasis on the original site where it was founded. The original *polis* was confined, ordered, oriented according to the path of the sun, proud of its individuality and its culture. In the last five centuries it has evolved into an overflowing physical body, dense, "porous," multicultural and, in recent times, also strongly multiethnic. It is a body that is often contradictory, marked by pomp and misery, by differences and contrasts, by catastrophes and vital recoveries. Seen from afar, it has always seemed to be a city of unrepeatable beauty: "it is easy to love Naples from the sea," it has often been said. But if one penetrates the interior, the city reveals itself to be disquieting, captivating and repellent, hospitable and impenetrable, wretched and rich, simultaneously tormented and aware.

"In reality it is gray: a red-ocher gray, a white-gray. It is very gray compared to the sky and the sea.... The city is rocky. From above, out of reach from the sound of voices, seen from Castel San Martino, it appears dead in the twilight, one with the rock. A slight strip of beach appears, with buildings thronging behind, one upon another.... The architecture is porous like this rock. Buildings and actions are transformed, one into the other, in courtyards, arcades, stairways. Everything is given the latitude to become a theater of new constellations, never seen before. The definitive, the codified is avoided.... Thus the architecture emerges, an essential example of the community's rhythm. Civilized, private and well ordered only in the grand hotels—and in the warehouses of the port—anarchic, contorted and rustic at the center, where only fifty years ago large stretches of road were inserted, and only in these is the house the cell of urban architecture in a northern sense. Within it, however, the block of dwellings is held together at the corners by images of the Madonna on the walls, almost as if they were iron clips." Until a short time ago, this is how the city was vividly perceived and profoundly misunderstood by European intellectuals (the quote is from Walter Benjamin and Asja Lacis, 1924).

Over the centuries Naples has oscillated between two destinies. Its pre-Greek roots, which date back to the seventh century B.C., hold the origins of a millennial vocation, strictly tied to the sea. But the Greek colonization in the fifth century B.C. the city back from the sea, confirming its position on terra firma, seeking nourishment not only from the waters, but above all from the land. It thus created the premise for a "geo-metry," a terrestrial measuring of the city, which would endure at length. After two thousand years, the Spanish and Baroque city once again looked out over the sea, and its urban body, remixing an idea of earth, water, and fire, became kneaded and magmatic. In the eighteenth century the Enlightenment and Bourbon city once again focused its imagination on geometry and on the land; it withdrew from the sea to the point where it dreamed of duplicating itself to the north, in the interior, in the city of Caserta, and produced a destination for European capital parallel to that of its sister cities, London and Paris. But by the late eighteenth century, after the inexorable divergence between north and south created by the industrial revolution, the city reproposed its original Mediterranean destiny, in modern rather than archaic forms. Naples then moved closer to its other sister cities: Marseilles, Barcelona, Athens, Cairo, and Algiers.

The theme of the aristocratic residence in Naples must be seen within the context of this history. We must begin by understanding how this nearly two-thousand-year-old fabric of memories and forms encountered and clashed with the typology of the noble palace, which came from Renaissance Florence and Rome. This occurred when the Aragonese court, in the fifteenth century, sanctioned the construction of this type of building and then, in the following century, when the Neapolitan aristocracy began to abandon its landed estates and move to the city.

To understand the specific characteristics of the aristocratic residence in Naples we must focus, preliminarily, on the specific identity of the city. It is an identity that is very complex and, above all, very present in the lives of its inhabitants. Over the course of centuries, this identity has played a leading role in the definition of spaces and has made it difficult to concentrate on the architecture of individual buildings. Naples places a certain burden on its buildings, smothering the structures, expanding the details, embracing and suffocating them, corroding and restraining them, without ever checking their abusive development, but, at the same time, forcing them to grow upon themselves and thus to infinitely preserve their roots in the subsoil. In fact, the noble residence, particularly from the sixteenth century onward, interweaves a dialogue with the city. This dialogue is anything but peaceful; rather, it is a sort of duel, a struggle for predominance, made of adaptations and oppressions, attacks and defenses, public ostentation and spasmodic investigations of private corners of paradise removed from the city, a territory belonging to all but for the exclusive enjoyment of the few. Within this history the city appears as a large maternal body, with everyone together and with no one, a body that can be plundered for the pleasure of the strongest, for their own advantage. At the same time, it is always urgent, weighing down with its material, its crowds, its sounds, its odors, and it always, sooner or later, holds its palaces and its villas in a crushing embrace.

Images of the city's origins: *Ulysses and the Sirens*, Attic storage jar from Vulci, 6th-5th century B.C. (London, British Museum).

Vocations and Destinies

The name "Napoli" offers clues to the city's history. *Nea* means new, while *polis* means collective, organized, fortified habitation. Thus the name indirectly indicates that it replaced an earlier city, an "old" city (a *palae-polis*), the name and substance of which have been lost.

The Neapolis that the Greeks established in the fifth century B.C. was an urban settlement, laid out in precise fashion, with a clearly designed interior. It had an enclosing wall and was oriented to the path of the sun. But this solar city was meant to annul the presence of an earlier "dark" city, founded barely two centuries before, along the water's edge. That earlier settlement lacked defined form or clear boundaries, and its only reference was the orientation of the earth toward the sea. Through Strabo's historical accounts, we know that this older city, or *palaepolis*, was called Parthenope. The name tells us that the city was dedicated to one of the three sirens, ancient divinities of the sea driven out by the luminous advent of Greek civilization. According to myth, the sirens had unchallenged dominion over the Mediterranean until Odysseus, a solar hero, was able to conquer their power through the exercise of his exquisitely human powers of reason. Their petrified bodies, washed ashore along the Tyrrhenian sea, are the origins of certain sacred sites in Campania and Calabria.

Thus in the founding myth for Naples/Parthenope, we find the theme of a double identity: human/divine, solar/sea. The reestablishment of the city also testifies to a profound reestablishment of the imagination, indicating the emergence of the Mediterranean world from myth and its entry into history. Between the seventh and the fifth century B.C. the cult of the sirens, whose vestiges can be detected in the Mediterranean along the extremely ancient metal trade routes, was abandoned. The worship of that hybrid divinity, represented in animal-human and male-female forms, was replaced by a sun cult (Apollonian, male), with its commemorative corollaries of knowledge (the cults of Athena and of the Sibyls, bearers of Apollo's oracle).

Thus living in Naples means facing an eternal duality, engaging in an original conflict (in myth these take the forms of a siren and a hero, from the waters of the sea and from the light of the sun), aligned *against* but also *next to* each other. This dates back to the unresolved duality at the city's foundation, between order and chaos, civil rule and untamable wild impulses.

These extremely ancient dynamics have been impressed, as into a cast, on the architecture of the city as it has taken shape over the millennia.

Rules

The solar city of Neapolis was built in the fifth century B.C. according to an orthogonal street plan common to cities established by the Greeks in the Mediterranean. During this same period, this type of plan was perfected and systematized in Greece by Hippodamus of Miletus. (Thus it is erroneous to define the layout of Naples as "Hippodamian"—a frequent mistake—since its origins are more archaic and, in any case, the city plan could not have come under the immediate influence of developments occurring in Greece at the same time.) This plan uses an abstract system of urban organization, and its enduring influence has traversed the millennia, up to our own time. Even today, the historic center of Naples, which we now call the "ancient center," reveals its original design intact. And over the centuries, it was stronger than any social change or any stylistic innovation. It thus fundamentally influenced all architectural constructions in the city, in their forms, dimensions, and reciprocal relationships.

The city's original layout was based on a geometric principle that can be defined generally as "projective": a theoretical rule of organization of the land that exclusively covers the forms and proportions of spaces, apart from their physical appropriation by the structures that will occupy them and those structures' material characteristics. This layout assigned a *rectilinear scheme* and *directions* to the city's streets, and thus determined the look of future construction. The main direction was east-west; the other, secondary direction, north-south. Thus in the fifth century B.C. the urban fabric was configured, once and for all, from the orthogonal scheme of *plateiai* and *stenopoi*: "broad streets" and "narrow streets." Or, in Latin, these are the *decumani* and the *cardines*: "streets that intersect like an X" (X is, of course, the Roman numeral for *decem*, or ten) and "hinge streets." The basic layout of the city was made up of three *decumani* and seventeen *cardines*. This "projective" principle was supplemented by a "Euclidean" geometric principle. This second rule was still abstract but invested the spaces with *scale*. It assigned specific dimensions to buildable lots (*insulae* in Latin), cut out along the ground by the streets, creating a particular shape, an elongated rectangle. This gave a specific physiognomy to the city and ingrained in its inhabitants a

Images of the city's origins: a sculpture group, the "Body of Naples," now located along the *decumanus inferior* of Graeco-Roman Naples. A Roman copy of a Hellenistic original, probably executed in the 2nd century after Christ, it was discovered during construction in the 12th century. An allegory of the Nile River, it represents abundance.

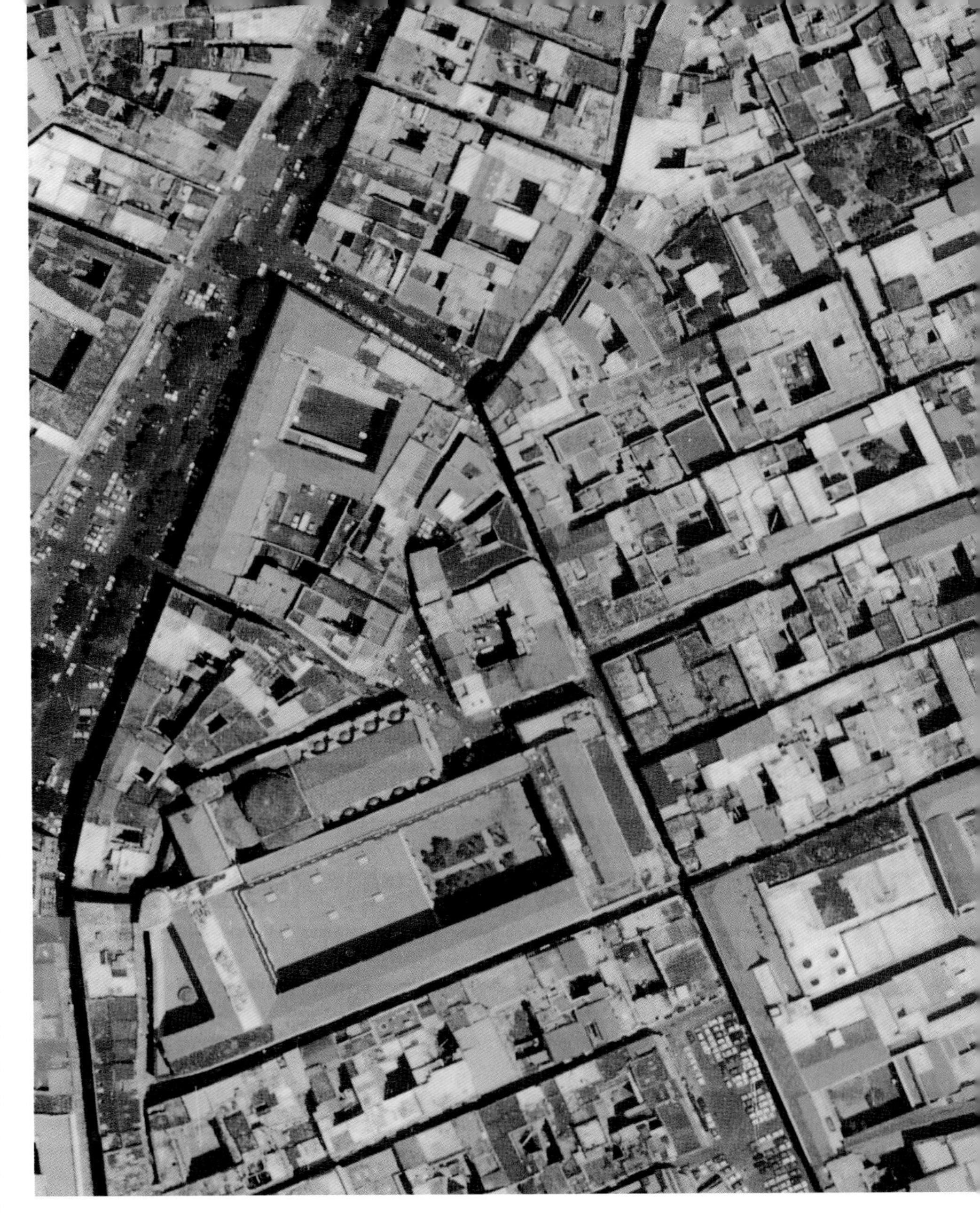

Neapolis, the solar city: aerial view of the ancient center of Naples.

habit—gradually consolidated until it became ineradicable—for constricted spaces, narrow streets, buildings pressed close together, an absence of piazzas. These elements would be reproduced over time and in the new neighborhoods, even when, during a process of more or less controlled expansion, the city went beyond the boundaries of the original walls.

During the period of Graeco-Roman development, this primary grid created an urban plan schematized by a division into theoretically equivalent parts. Then, during the Middle Ages, a system of functional "stresses" was superimposed that altered the homogeneity of the initial layout. This was the system of *seggi*, or seats, territorial divisions that stemmed from the regrouping of family constellations, often unified under a single surname, around a local meeting place for representatives of the group. The urban fabric, while remaining formally uniform, became less homogeneous functionally and symbolically in terms of centers of prestige and power. The five *seggi* (Capuana, Montagna, Nido, Porto, and Portanova) developed a new "topological" geometry, overlaid upon the original projective-Euclidean geometry. This "topological" organization was no longer abstract, but very concrete in its organization of space: it was tied directly to sites and to processes of physical appropriation of the urban plan by the inhabitants. This rule, which left intact the shape and size of the *insulae*, introduced new criteria of relationship: the perception of relationships of inclusion/exclusion, continuity/discontinuity, adjacency, order, "values" of the elements of inhabited space. All this occurred, however, without questioning the general form of the city as a walled enclosure organized internally by the regularity of the street layout. Instead, a system of internal transgressions was created.

During the Middle Ages, this was the origin of a double system of constraints within the confined body of the city. On the one hand, there was constriction within a rigid formal and dimensional scheme, confined by the enclosing wall, regulated by the rectilinear and orthogonal layout of the streets and by the size of the *insulae*, narrow in the east-west direction and elongated in the north-south direction. On the other hand, the shift of political power to Castelnuovo—which brought much of the resident aristocracy with it, toward the western zone of the city—and the incorporation of new business communities (people from Amalfi, Scala, Genoa, Catalonia) near the port, and finally the leading role that places of worship in the ancient city came to play, all contributed to the creation of new hierarchies within the plan. These shifts also introduced the idea of free appropriation and regrouping of space, depending on poles of interest.

This was the urban fabric within which, in the fifteenth and sixteenth centuries, the palaces of Naples began to be constructed. Without an understanding of the conflict between coexisting different and heterogeneous rules of organization, one cannot explain the specific metamorphosis that the "palazzo" building type has undergone in this city. Without this interpretive key—namely a recognition of the leading role played by an almost two-thousand-year-old urban entity, rich in internal contrasts—one cannot understand why, unlike other large Italian cities such as Rome and Florence, in most cases even luxury dwellings in Naples assume a resultant form, permeated by space, rather than a finalized form that generates space.

Palazzo Gravina, now the School of Architecture.

"Palatium"

In its very name, the building type of the "palazzo"—"a grand, aristocratic building"— preserves the memory of an imperial prototype and a compact, solid, prominent form. But really it is strongly modeled and modified by pressures transmitted by an urban body like that of Naples—dense, stratified, complex.

Palatium originally referred to the name of the Palatine, one of the seven hills of ancient Rome. The term derives from the pre-Indo-European word *pala*, which signifies "rotundity." It was only later that the meaning of the word changed, through that process of transference of meaning from a primary object to adjacent objects, a process defined as "metonymy" in rhetoric. In this case the transference of meaning was from the hill to the imperial building that was built upon it. Thus the core meaning of "palazzo" is an essentially compact and elevated masonry building, with the impressiveness of a hill. This is why, in the Middle Ages, the "palazzi" par excellence were public buildings, such as the Palazzo della Signoria in Florence and the Palazzo Ducale in Venice. In the Renaissance they were private buildings, such as the Palazzo Strozzi in Florence, the Palazzo Farnese in Rome: solid architecture, stabile, parallelepipeds, rising clearly from the ground, with perpendicular angles, outlined against the sky with the broken line of their crenellated towers, or with the straight or broken line of their cornices. This architecture was representative of the laic, terrestrial, productive nature of the new class emerging in the urban centers (or *borghi*): the bourgeoisie. The "palazzo" type refers to an architectural object that is intended to play a leading role, creating around itself a cubic space, organized according to an orthogonal grid of length-width-depth. Homogeneous among themselves, the palazzi are clearly measurable because they are proportioned to the "human scale." Moreover, the type was developed in urban contexts (sixteenth-century Florence and Rome, for example) that were being designed at the same time, according to the same poetics, through the use of the theoretical-practical tool of perspective, with the layout of visual axes, vanishing points, breadths and distances where the glance could be directed.

But what happened in Florence and Rome could not occur in Naples. The urban fabric had remained extremely dense over the millennia. It was established on Graeco-Roman street plans that did not exceed five to seven meters in width and generally did not allow for piazzas, with rare exceptions in the form of widened areas tangential to the street. The passage from an impenetrable, tactile city to one that was spread out and visual, a transition that marked the Renaissance in architecture of the cities of central Italy, would

Palazzo Sanseverino, now the church of Gesù Nuovo.

have been impossible in fifteenth- and sixteenth-century Naples, except in rare instances. Even after antiquity and the Middle Ages, all the buildings in Naples—through force of habit, because of the hilly conditions of the land, because of a lack of large-scale planning, because of acquisitive life styles—continued to crowd together, to compete, shoulder to shoulder. There was little space, and buildings were placed one opposite another, face to face. Moreover, beginning with the period directly inspired by Florence, it was rare for Neapolitan palaces to have unified facades. This occurs only occasionally (Palazzo Penne, Palazzo Carafa di Maddaloni, Palazzo Marigliano) and when the street widens in front of the building (Palazzo Orsini di Gravina, now the School of Architecture, which overlooks the Largo Monteoliveto or the Palazzo Sanseverino, later transformed into the Chiesa del Gesù Nuovo, which overlooks the piazza of the same name).

Isabella di Resta quoted a visitor, Giulio Cesare Capaccio, in a text written in the form of a dialogue on early-seventeenth-century Naples:

> F: "...do you know what seems to me to be missing?" C: "What would that be?" F: "The beauty of the buildings. I have seen those of Rome, Florence, Genoa, Venice, which are magnificent, well built, with a design that is enchanting, that pleases the eyes, and in a splendor of nobility, acquaints you with the grandeur of those who live there. In Naples one feels the lack of this... as well as the buildings. I have seen a few, which I could count on one hand, that have some appearance of nobility." C: "It's all true and I know what you mean; the house of the Prince of Salerno... that of Ferdinando Orsino Duke of Gravinathat of Fabricio di Sangro...." F: "...others are comfortable but are not architecture."

Only the Palazzo Reale, in 1600, would have the true privilege of being able to be admired frontally from a distance. The only piazza in Naples that has perspectival breadth (Largo di Palazzo, later Foro Murat, the present-day Piazza del Plebiscito) was laid out opposite the palace's west facade. Throughout the seventeenth century, Naples also lacked an architecture of palace facades. For the most part, instead of a unified design, which would have been difficult to perceive in the absence of distant views, there were spectacular ornaments, which accentuated the architecture's plastic elements. Foremost was the entrance, surmounted by the family coat of arms, which became a metaphor for the entire palace and its social and symbolic values. Then there were balconies, rustication, and cornices. A facade entirely composed as a function of the exterior space would appear only after the mid-eighteenth century, the Palazzo Doria d'Angri being the only one, after the old Palazzo Carafa di

Maddaloni, with the good fortune to arise isolated between two side streets. But generally, a view of architectural forms was not able to prevail over the din of sounds, contacts, odors, and pressures, which held sway in the street. No single building was able to establish a position of dominance.

Backdrops

The most conspicuous flowering of noble palaces in Naples appeared as a consequence of profound social changes brought about between 1532 and 1553 by the policies of Viceroy Pedro da Toledo. With a great abundance of detail and meticulous documentary reconstruction, Gérard Labrot has recorded what was a true uprooting of the aristocracy from its original landed estates. This was done by the viceroy in order to draw the nobility into court life and to make them respectful of that existence. But for the aristocracy, Pedro da Toledo's plan, using the enticements of the court, was a tragic trap, because it deceptively provided "the enclosure within which their wealth was exhausted in construction projects, their rebellious energies were worn down by rancorous neighborhood rivalries and their pretenses were gratified in emulative onslaughts." Thus the nobility's construction of urban residences, which progressively replaced their principal dwellings, whether ancient castles or provincial palaces on their estates, dissipated tensions that would have been unleashed against the centralized authority of the Spanish viceroyalty, had the aristocracy's proud territorial autonomy continued. Their architecture also came to constitute a materialization of vanity, arrogance, envy, and exhibitionism, as spectacular as it was a sign of their own lack of true power, whether by choice or necessity.

We have examined the original conditions that fostered development of palace architecture in Naples during the fifteenth and at the dawn of the sixteenth century. Now we need to follow the evolution of conditions provided by the urban spatial context into which subsequent and much more numerous constructions of this type were inserted.

An examination of early views of Naples (the *Tavola Strozzi*, a fifteenth-century painted panel depicting a view of Naples from the sea; a bird's-eye view in an engraving by Étienne Dupérac and Antonio Lafréry, 1566; a pen drawing by Jan Van

The *Tavola Strozzi*, 15th century (Naples, Capodimonte Museum).

Stinemolen, 1582) reveals how, until and throughout the sixteenth century, the city continued to be perceived and represented with the original characteristics of a *polis*. It was seen as an enclosed and well-organized settlement, with clearly identified boundaries: toward the sea, the coast with the port; toward the hinterlands, the fortified silhouette of the hills. It is also obvious how, in the Renaissance, the enclosing wall became more rigid. For strategic reasons, walls were reinforced and the number of urban castles increased. These were great, masculine examples of architecture designed for war, which allowed dominion over the space both inside and outside the city. In these castles, the military function was separated definitively from the royal residential function (which was shifted to the heart of the city). The city boundary was transformed from a defensive membrane into a splendid carapace. Thus, until the early seventeenth century (Alessandro Baratta's engraving of 1629 showing a grand perspectival view comes to mind), an enclosed, well-ordered, fortified Naples was recognizable above all by the emergence of a specific piece of architecture: the Castel Sant'Elmo, on the summit of the hill rising to the north, opposite the sea. This iconography of the city found its most complete and effective expression in an engraving by Bastiaen Stopendaal, from 1653, where Naples appears crowned by an extremely beautiful helmet, with a crest adorned with a windblown banner. In a more military view, engraved by C. Danckerts in 1660, the layout of the basic urban physiognomy is entrusted, significantly, to only two features: the enclosing wall and the castle on the hill.

Chronicles show that during the course of the sixteenth century, and even before the urban iconography revealed it, there was a feeling that a profound, irreversible change was taking place in the city, one that was occurring behind its age-old exterior.

Pedro da Toledo's urban plan gave an area outside the walls a westward direction, from Monteoliveto to Montesanto and Chiaia and the hill of Pizzofalcone. In the first half of the century urban development pushed toward the hills, opening a period of great expansion and building activity. As urban development spread to the slopes of the hills, particularly the Pizzofalcone (the ancient Monte Echia of the primitive acropolis of Parthenope), this plan induced a profound change

top right
Antonio Lafréry, *Bird's-eye View of Naples*, engraving by Stefano Dupérac, 1566 (Naples, San Martino Museum).

opposite
Alessandro Baratta, *Bird's-eye View of Naples*, engraving, 1629 (Rome, Banca Commerciale Italiana).

below
Bastiaen Stopendaal, *Bird's-eye View of Naples*, engraving, 1653 (Naples, San Martino Museum).

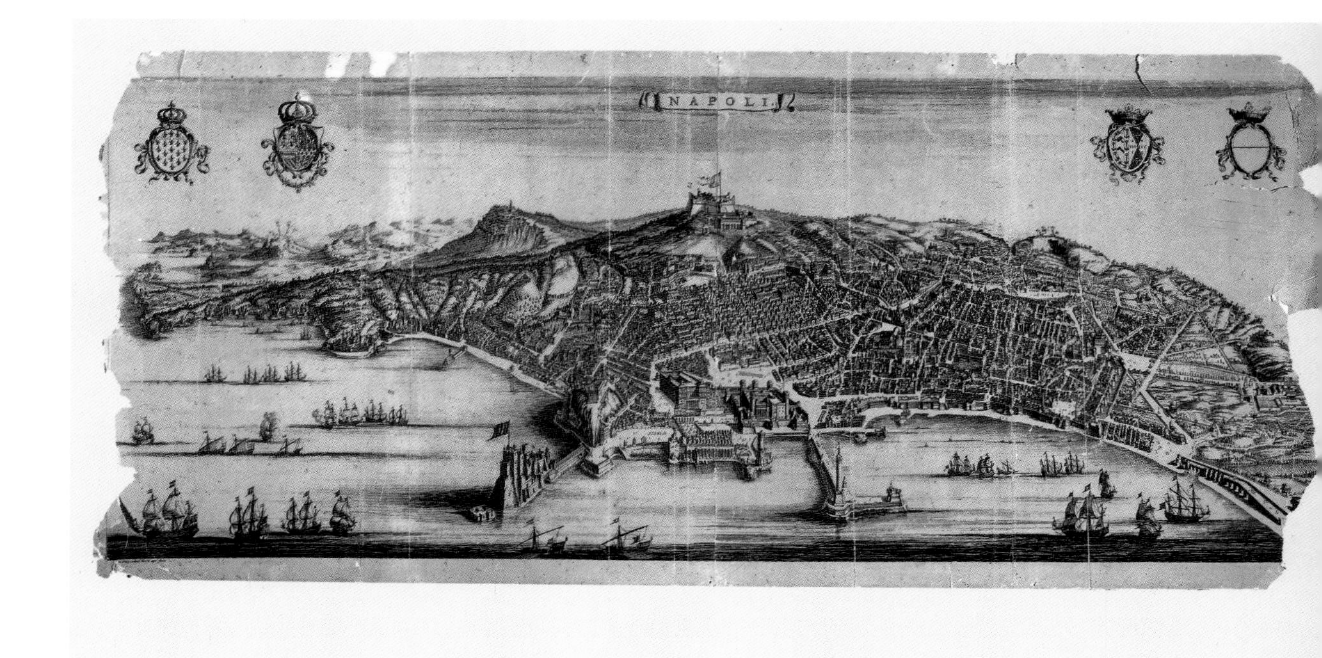

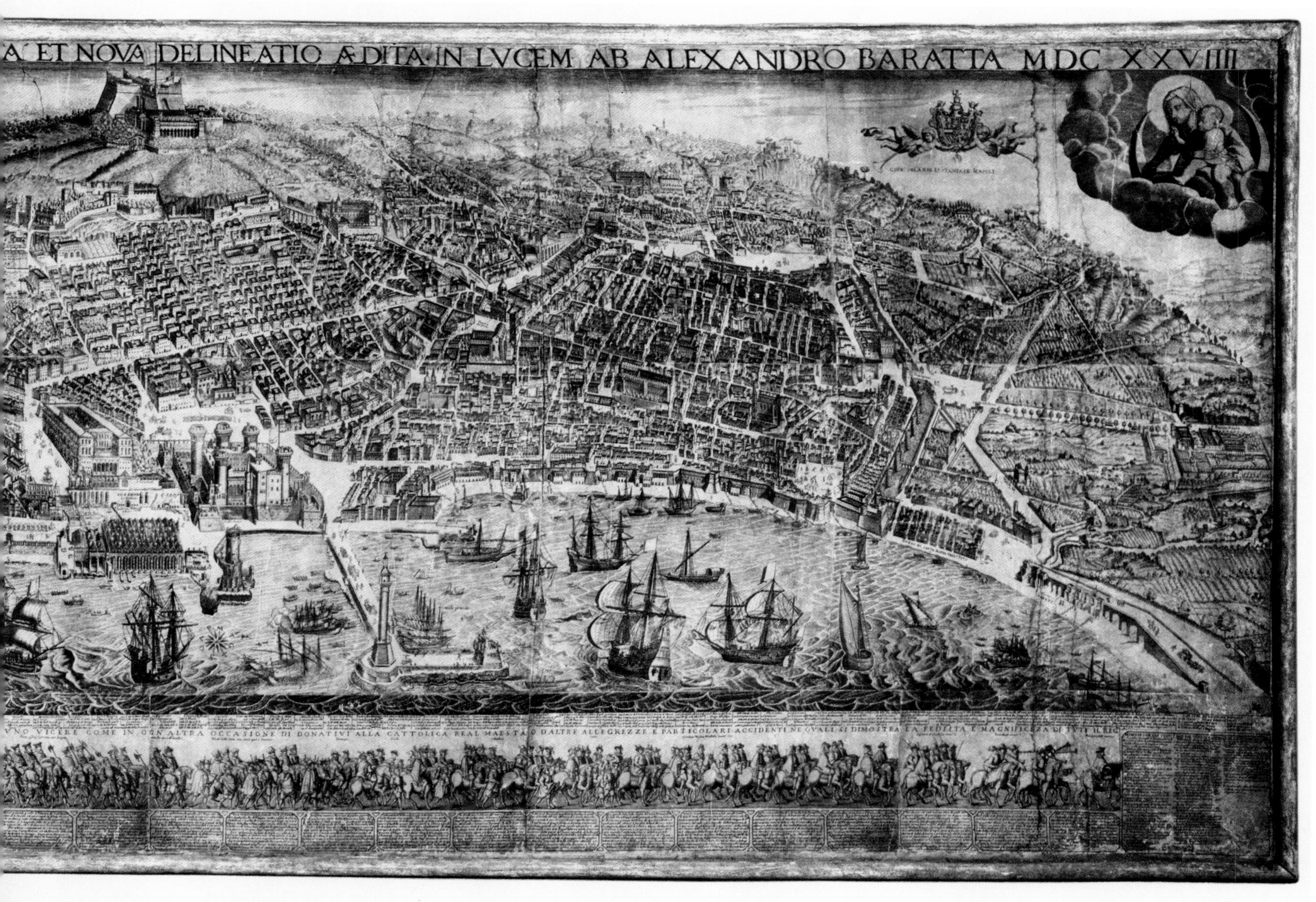
A ET NOVA DELINEATIO ÆDITA IN LVCEM AB ALEXANDRO BARATTA MDC XXVIIII

of perception of the space within the city. For the first time, the *image of the sea* entered that perception, as a backdrop for the urban view.

It is important to remember that Neapolis, the enclosed and well-organized solar city, had arisen in opposition to the original Parthenope, which, with neither defined form nor enclosing wall, simply looked out over the water, taking advantage of the natural form of the promontory of Monte Echia. The new city showed a propensity to distance itself from the sea, withdrawing inland and eastward, into a mainland area where it could entirely control its own plan with geometric criteria. Pedro da Toledo's plan returned to that earlier orientation, assumed at the time of the city's origin. It pushed the city westward and had it once again look outward toward the sea. It is easy to understand how this shift, which cut into and modified the roots—imaginative as well as physical—of the city's primitive founding, triggered a profound change in the nature of urban spaces, which could be much more capacious than those conceived on the basis of solely rational and technical requirements. The first consequence was a general weakening of the city's Apollonian and solar (that is, rational) qualities. Then the city's body and image reintegrated more ancient, prerational, prehistoric qualities, closer to the nature of the sea. Going back to mythical language, we might say that over the course of the sixteenth century, the conditions were prepared for water (which leads to fusion) to powerfully gain the upper hand over light (which leads to separation).

During the sixteenth century, at the same time as the first large urban aristocratic palaces were being built, many disturbing signs unequivocally pointed to the weakening of the city's boundaries. These boundaries diminished and then shifted, first southward, where they dissolved in the water, merging with the edge of the sea (although in the meantime, to the east, dramatic and spectacular rustic outcroppings were about to appear, without warning, like new—and terrible—actors of the imaginary).

Throughout the sixteenth century, the edge of the sea was an area of transgression and provocation. Roberto Pane describes many accounts from that time. Antonio Bulifon mentions many horrid and curious spectacles that took place along the Posillipo walk: battles between dogs and cats, expositions of dwarfs, hangings of thieves. D. Confuorto describes the "spectacle" presented by the madness of the Marchesa di Petrella. Pirate raids sometimes reached as far as the beach of Mergellina. The San Vincenzo pier, begun in the early seventeenth century, remained unfinished.

The culmination of this process, forty years later, would be the construction of a palace that arose "*'nu pede 'nfuso e n'auto asciutto*" ("one foot wet and another dry," that is, half in the sea, half on land), sanctioning the emergence of an ambiguity between what was inside and what was outside the city, what was land and what was sea, what was civilization and what was nature. This was the Palazzo Donn'Anna, and it too was to remain unfinished.

Between the sixteenth and the seventeenth century, the entire boundary of the city was weakened and revealed disturbing breaches. According to Capaccio, while "elsewhere one sees nothing but guards, sentinels, doors closed at night with extreme diligence, [in Naples] day and night, these are seen open, nor does one notice any wood or iron material that might close them."

All these signs of the progressive decay of the boundaries actually presaged a century of catastrophes.

> 1632: the eruption of Vesuvius. In the middle of the night on Monday, we heard a considerable earthquake... at the top of the mountain there was a very great fire, and it grew moment by moment, taking a double path. Part rose skyward with such velocity that in a brief time it had gone beyond the height of all the clouds, and part spread out in layers down the mountain like a river.... When the sun came out Tuesday morning what at night had looked like a red-hot river, with the new light of day seemed like a cloud rising from the earth, straight up, to the seventh region of the air, and then expanded in such a way that the part that rose straight up resembled a thick trunk of a very tall pine tree, and the other upper portion, spread all around, seemed like an immense pine cone, more vast than a very large mountain. News spread that the river that wound along the ground had burned men and flocks, farms and houses.... There was no one who didn't think they would die that night" (from a letter describing Vesuvius, written by Giov. Battista Manzo in Naples to Antonio Burni in Rome, 19 October 1631).

Domenico Gargiulo, known as Micco Spadaro, *The Killing of Don Giuseppe Carafa during the Masaniello Revolt of 1647* (Naples, San Martino Museum).

Salvator Rosa, *Humana fragilitas*
(Cambridge, Fitzwilliam Museum).

This first terrestrial catastrophe (followed, during the seventeenth century, by the earthquakes of 1688 and 1694) violently brought to the forefront the destructive power of Vesuvius in terms that had not been experienced since the year 79, the date of the mythic eruption that had destroyed Pompeii and Herculaneum. The lava reached the height of the Ponte della Maddalena, the eastern edge of Naples. According to accounts from the time, it was stopped only by the "intervention" of San Gennaro, who is said to have appeared in the sky, amid the clouds, and was seen by a crowd of some 300,000 people. Painters such as Scipione Compagno and Domenico Gargiulo, otherwise known as Micco Spadaro, depict an insidious mixture of horror at the catastrophe, religious exaltation, and spectacular fascination that the event provoked. *The Procession of 17 December 1631* by Gargiulo portrays a crowd of poor people simply watching the apocalyptic action that terrestrial and divine deities (opportunely represented by political and ecclesiastical authorities) enacted between earth and sky, on the city stage.

For a long century thereafter, a constant threat of chaos and death seemed to loom over the city. 1647: the revolt of Masaniello. 1656: a plague epidemic. In his paintings, Micco Spadaro merges the two episodes, representing them as different death scenes in the theater of the city. Even more obviously, Carlo Coppola represents the disasters of the plague in a theatrical urban space constructed in central perspective, where the palaces of the city act as theater wings and Vesuvius forms the backdrop. Salvator Rosa allegorically examines *Humana fragilitas*. The theme of death and decay aroused fear and horror, but also curiosity and a sort of morbid pleasure. An aristocratic taste for collecting developed that found amusement in macabre objects. One of these, a wax model known by the title *La Scandalosa*, by an unknown artist, depicts with horrendous crudeness a woman's face devoured by the decomposition of death.

Life entered death, death entered life, and a rule regarding the separation of opposites was broken, a rule that is also basic to classic city planning.

During the seventeenth century the city thus lost its most profound security, but instead of building itself anew, it began to create a fiction in order to reassure itself. The worship of San Gennaro in the streets, with the ritual of the miracle of the periodic flowing of blood and the silver statue carried in processions, is the theatricalization of a relationship with the forces of chaos. No plans were proposed for the improvement of hygiene or social reorganization, and instead the city was abandoned to fate, religion, and the irrational. Machines for festivals, processional apparatuses, shrines, spires, and gallows function as set designs. They were elaborate and emphatic masks for an ephemeral urban plan that filled the ever-growing void left by the inability (or lack of will) to come up with new criteria of order for a city that was subject to grave danger and suffering on a grand scale.

This entire expressive jumble makes it clear how Naples, at this point, had lost its connection to the millennial quality of a *polis* without elaborating new, more modern certainties. It is also clear that a metamorphosis was taking place, inverse to the founding process, a true undoing: a regression from the discrete to the continuous, from order to disorder, from the controllable to the uncontrollable. An iconological reading of the images that celebrate the city confirm this regression. Unlike in Renaissance tradition, the city is no longer represented from south to north, that is, in the diffused and serene light generated by a position of the sun to one's back. The image of the city is more focused on human constructions; the viewpoint shifts, goes westward or eastward where, in either case, it frames the city against the backdrop of a volcanic landscape and a sky blinded by the sun on the horizon. Jan Van Essen's famous mid-seventeenth-century depiction of Naples from the sea shows precisely this moment of transition. The scene is still partially constructed according to sixteenth-century tradition, as a view of the city from the sea, centered on Castel Sant'Elmo. But at the right, at the cost of considerable perspectival distortion, Vesuvius appears, a grand symbol of nature, unyielding to man, pushing to enter the scene and the image of the city.

Then the iconography of the city becomes gloomy. In the mid-seventeenth century, Didier Barra and François de Nomé (confused in historiography until forty years ago, under a single name, the mysterious Monsù Desiderio) still represent a dark city, the murky sky pierced by flashes of lightening, seen from the south and east, looking westward.

Aided once again by Roberto Pane's wonderful descriptions, we can imagine a city where the glance no longer followed the path of the sun but encountered darkness. The space of the city was dominated by sounds: processional songs, stentorian proclamations, the rifle shots of executions, the ringing of church bells of the congregation of the *Bianchi* political faction, entrusted with offering religious assistance to the condemned, the sing-song calls of strolling vendors: *bastasi* (porters), *bazzarioti* (peddlers), sellers of bran, tripe, snow, biscuits, wood, flax, oil, chicken, ricotta, cheese, pastries....

This is the context in which the building of aristocratic palaces in Naples flourished.

Let us examine, then, what happened to the architecture of these buildings.

In the city, which was gradually deconstructed and made to open outward, with its boundaries becoming ineffective, buildings were subject to a double type of pressure.

On the one hand, in opposition to expansion beyond the walls, the city became increasingly internalized. Forced too long to remain within the old walls (by periodic prohibitions issued by the Spanish viceroys against construction beyond), squeezed by privileges granted to expanding church construction projects, wedged in the double system of obligations inherited from the Graeco-Roman layout and from the medieval urban topology, building could not help but grow inward and on itself, incorporating preexisting structures, greatly increasing in height along the ancient road network, making the city more and more like a labyrinth. The sun, principal point of reference for the city's original orientation, no longer entered the streets. The city's interior began to acquire that visceral quality that, in 1884, Matilde Serao described—quoting Émile Zola—as "il ventre di Napoli" (the belly of Naples). Palaces could not be isolated, nor could they greatly expand, and so they sought to *appear* unique and grand, adopting the devices necessary to fictitiously impose their prestige on the urban scene.

At the same time, between the late sixteenth and the early seventeenth century, the sale of monastic lands lying outside the city created conditions for the construction of new aristocratic dwellings, more spacious and grander in scale, because they were not subject to the compression of the ancient fabric of the city. And the competition that ensued between nobility "of the district" and nobility "outside the district" provided further stimulus to architectural ostentation in these new palaces.

On the other hand, in the city that had lost its usual order, architectural rules also broke down. Parallel to the process of urban deconstruction, there was a general deregulation in relationships between technicians and their clients. In the frenetic production of aristocratic residences, which in any case never involved a totally new plan, but rather adaptations and remanipulations of preexisting buildings, local architects were for the most part overlooked, or consulted for only partial interventions and treated like servants. Thus the noble palaces were designed mostly in dilettante fashion by their owners. The process that Labrot calls "ontological irregularity" developed, and palaces became palimpsests, "ineffectual *bricolages* that produce bizarre, but also delightful, results." Consequently "unfinished, suspended, the Neapolitan palace appears only rarely as a *work*." And "the reproduction throughout the entire city of this ambitious, impulsive, both fascinating and disheartening architecture, arouses a feeling of general instability, of disorder. Entropy seriously threatens everything."

Thus a unified building type did not exist. These palaces were heterogeneous, composite, spread out. They were constructions that grew at different tempos and in different styles, depending on need and the availability of resources. Nor was there a separate and distinct function between the interior of the building and the exterior of the street, but rather an interpenetration of different uses, which turned ground floors and mezzanine levels into labyrinthine tangles of workshops, carriage houses, and working-class dwellings. These existed in the shelter of the aristocratic residence, disdainfully and defensively placed on the *piano nobile*. There were no facades unified by codified architectural orders or classical symmetry, but a confusion of emphatic elements, arranged with a display of arrogance, ostentation, and power.

The entire traditional value of the facade was reemployed and subsumed by a single element: the entrance. Let us quote

Domenico Antonio Vaccaro, *Palazzo Spinelli di Tarsia*, engraving (Naples, Società di Storia Patria).

Labrot once again: "A formidable machine that invades the street, the entrance rises up to increasingly extraordinary heights, on robust columns or exuberant piers, frenetic, carved pediments, sometimes to the limits of delirium.... The entrance is the palace itself, triumphal arch and tabernacle, space and image of the owner: it presents and represents... it is the anticipation of Difference, pushed to excess."

The compression exercised by the urban context determined a true perspectival anamorphosis of the facade, which was negated and entirely reestablished in the gigantic entrances. The framework for the entrance was distorted in an effort to capture attention and impose a sense of authority. In a city of transgressions and excess, one can well understand how, in the architecture of aristocratic palaces, two separate demands—defense and theatricality—were increasingly asserted.

The distortion of the facade was accompanied by an implosion that produced a sort of "swallowing up" of the urban space by the building itself. The expanse that was denied the external facade, due to lack of street space or a piazza, was created within, in an expansion and concatenation of related spaces (entrance halls, courtyards, stairways, interior gardens). The result was often that of an inverse telescoped perspective; the natural sequence of entry, which would lead from an exterior beyond the threshold, passing through the entrance toward the building's interior, was replaced by a paradoxical sequence that proceeded in opposite fashion, from the interior of the building, toward an exterior that seemed to lie beyond the building itself, but which often was purely virtual and fictitious. The Palazzo Acquaviva d'Atri, Palazzo Casamassima, and Palazzo Maddaloni offer the most significant examples of this skillful process of progressive revelation. Upon entering, one is allowed glimpses of an interior destination, but one that is newly open to the sky and thus full of light. This destination is presented as marvelous but unattainable, displayed, but from a distance, exhibited but arrogantly prohibited. This typology reached its true apotheosis during the first half of the following century, in the architecture of Ferdinando Sanfelice. However, the only great dialogue with the real external space of the landscape was tackled by Domenico Antonio Vaccaro, in the extraordinary articulation of the courtyard of the Palazzo Spinelli di Tarsia.

The fleeting image of the interior paradise of the palace, announced by the plastic emphasis of the entrance, was caught in a central perspectival view that could be seen only at the moment when one passed through the doorway, over the threshold. This completed the symbolic message and the splendors announced by the entrance, but vanished once again as soon as the visitor, limited to a tangential, never frontal, path to the palace, advanced along the facade, leaving the entrance first to the side, then behind.

In Hans Holbein the Younger's celebrated painting *The Ambassadors* (National Gallery, London), the frontal representation of the noble diplomats dressed in furs, velvets, and jewels is accompanied by a stretched and incomprehens-

Pierre-Jacques Volaire, *Eruption of Vesuvius from the Maddalena Bridge* (Naples, Capodimonte Museum).

ible shape. The viewer, struck by a sense of unease, turns back for one last glance and perceives that this shape, seen in strongly foreshortened perspective, is the representation of a skull, a secret messenger of death. Similarly, it is only a strongly foreshortened view, following the official, frontal view, that reveals the true, most profound and sincere message of these seventeenth-century Neapolitan palaces. Moving back through the entrance, having consumed the illusion presented in the frontal view, one enters the narrow, dark streets, but then looks back once more at the fictitious portal, and it becomes clear that these are *tragic* buildings. Behind their triumphant masks, they speak to us with torment about the fragility of life, the vanity of worldly things.

Giants

The political change brought about by the transition from the Spanish viceroyalty to the Bourbon reign marked a significant change in direction in the spatial organization of the city, and this was reflected in the construction of aristocratic residences. Let us once more follow this transformation through the evolution of the city's iconographic image.

Throughout the first half of the eighteenth century, images of Naples still document a landscape of border violations and catastrophes. Carlo Bonavia paints the fury of fire (*Eruption of Vesuvius*) and water (*Coastal View with Shipwreck*). A new viewpoint appears in representations of the city, one that is tangential, no longer at right angles, to the coast. The backdrop of the sea now appears as an element in the urban imagination, whether the view looks eastward or westward. For some time Vesuvius attracted European travelers, and foreign painters such as Thomas Wijck, Johannes Lingelbach, Charles Grenier de la Croix, Pierre-Jacques Volaire, and Michael Wutky were fascinated by its eruptions. They saw it as a spectacle capable of initiating a new aesthetic sense, distant from the sensual pleasure of "beauty," anticipating what would be a higher awareness of the "sublime." It was only in the second half of the eighteenth century, when the living memory of the eruptions and fire were muffled, that the image of the volcano begins to be tamed. Gradually progressing from the sublime to the picturesque, the image moves into the

The Albergo dei Poveri.

distance and becomes a large decorative contour behind the city. The paintings of Antonio Joli, Jean Houel, Philipp Hackert, Giovan Battista Lusieri, and William Turner show the Gulf of Naples as a basin of light. It no longer makes sense to look on land for the city's boundaries or criteria of order because the elements of the city and the landscape are integrated into a harmony that is no longer geometric but generally atmospheric. A new principle of order begins to appear in the city as a result of the nascent cultural sensitivity to the landscape, which creates the possibility for a new balance between interior and exterior: a balance no longer necessarily founded on the geometric control of territory but entrusted to the desire for a reciprocal dialogue between city and nature. The senses open up to the perception of new forms, and the mind expands to accommodate new images of space.

It is significant that foreigners contributed substantially to this renewal of a rustic iconography of the city. Indeed, during the eighteenth century, Naples—southern offshoot of Europe, stretched out over the Mediterranean—came to symbolize the final destination on the Grand Tour.

In the meantime, while playing this mythic role for Europe, Naples was able to construct an accurate representation of itself. The "precise" map created by Giovanni Carafa, duke of Noja, in 1775, goes beyond the old picturesque "bird's-eye" view and, for the first time, depicts the entire city in plan, that is, from a viewpoint located at an infinite distance.

In the great economic and social recovery of the Bourbon period, Naples became one of the places where the Enlightenment flourished, and the city assumed the role of the third capital of Europe, after London and Paris. An urban culture developed, and what had been an aesthetic issue became an ethical one as well, which involved not only architects but also intellectuals of various extractions, with contributions from the whole of Europe. This can be seen, for example, in descriptions of Naples by Goethe in *Italienische Reise* or in Meyer's *Darstellungen aus Italien*, as opposed to the idealized view expressed by Johann Gottfried Herder.

But it is precisely the development of accurate descriptions of the city that demonstrates, conversely, that it was becoming elusive in terms of direct experience. In a certain sense, the city was becoming unknown to its inhabitants and even its most cultivated visitors. Its material body was becoming too large, growing outward in all directions, exceeding those boundaries of three to four hundred meters that constitute the human eye's threshold of three-dimensional visibility and thus define the "human scale" of a settlement. For example, the city began to develop great axes of territorial penetration, toward Capua and Rome. These were elements that could be represented on a map but could not be encompassed within a pictorial view of the city, and it was no longer within the reach of architectural projects to control the city's expansion.

Enlightenment culture devised a new tool, the "plan," to control the city. This focused attention on the reinforcement of infrastructures, of connecting points within the urban fabric, but other built elements were left to their own fate. Architects returned to playing a role in the designing of spaces, but they were called in from outside, to exert "external," rigorous control over the city. Pasquale Belfiore has thoroughly analyzed how, in the eighteenth century, an "institutional" city was thus created, absorbing all attention and investment. This city increasingly assumed a grid plan, through which dark and forgotten areas began to appear, forming a parallel city of "remnants."

The following speaks for itself. In only twenty years, between 1730 and 1750, three gigantic architectural projects were designed for the city and its immediate surroundings. Two were royal: the Palazzo Reale in Capodimonte and the Palazzo Reale in Portici. Both, with large park complexes and woods surrounding them, incorporated whole sections of the landscape into the city, one on the hills in the immediate hinterland, the other on the eastern coast, along the slopes of Vesuvius. Their equally large-scale antithesis was the immense Albergo dei Poveri, designed by Ferdinando Fuga. This was to be a city within a building, the largest built structure in Europe. In some ways it was a mirror image of the magnificent palace of Caserta, which was being built at the same time by Luigi Vanvitelli, twenty kilometers to the north, to satisfy the Bourbon dream to transfer the capital there. The Albergo dei Poveri was supposed to contain five piazzas, an enormous church, and lodgings for all the poor of the realm; it was also meant to be a grand container of productive activity. No investment of any type was made where the poor really lived, in the working-class districts of the city, which escaped both the glance and thoughts of urban officialdom.

The Albergo dei Poveri, like the Palazzo Donn'Anna a century before, remained unfinished. But we can perhaps measure the gap between the utopia that generated it and what would have truly existed, had it been inhabited as planned. We can look at the outcome of the other immense building project of that period, which, although conceived with a different purpose, became in time a great collective dwelling for the poor and underprivileged: the Granili. Begun in 1779, also by Ferdinando Fuga, it was built along the edge of the sea, on the eastern coast of the city. It was meant to house the public granaries, military warehouses, and rope factories. Instead, inappropriately and abusively, it became a refuge for the homeless, a function that its more noble counterpart had been designed to fulfill, under legal sanction and with some forethought. The Granili also remained unfinished and no longer exists. This is how Anna Maria Ortese described it in 1953, in her story *La città involontaria*:

> It is a building some three hundred meters long, from fifteen to twenty meters wide, and much taller than that. For those who come upon it unexpectedly... it appears like a hill or a bald mountain, invaded by termites that run through it noiselessly and without any particular goal. In times past the walls were a dark red, which still emerges, here and there amid vast stains of yellows and smears of an equivocal green. I was able to count one hundred seventy-four openings in a single facade, of a breadth and height that modern taste would find extraordinary. Most portions are barred, there are some small terraces, and, at the back of the building, eight drainage pipes, which, attached to the third floor, slowly gush forth water along the silent wall. There are three floors, plus a ground level, hidden halfway below ground and protected by a ditch, and they include three hundred forty-eight rooms, all equally high and large, arranged in perfectly regular fashion, to the right and left of four hallways, one per floor, extending one kilometer and two hundred meters overall. Each hallway is illuminated by no more than twenty-eight light bulbs, five watts each. The width of each hallway ranges from seven to eight meters, and thus the word hallway designates, more than anything, four streets of some urban zone, raised up like the floors on a bus, and without any roof at all. For the ground floor and the two upper floors especially, sunlight is represented by those twenty-eight electric light bulbs, which shine weakly here, day and night. Eighty-six doors of private dwellings open onto the two sides of each hallway, forty-three to the right, forty-three to the left, plus one door for a toilet, distinguished by a series of numbers that go from one to three hundred forty-eight. Each of these spaces holds one to five families, with an average of three families per room. There are three thousand people living in the complex

Villa Acton Pignatelli and, in the background, the Castello Aselmeyer.

following page
Giacinto Gigante, *Naples from Conocchia* (Naples, private collection).

overall, divided into five hundred seventy families, with an average of six people per family. When three, four or five families live together in the same space, the density reaches twenty-five or thirty inhabitants per room.... It isn't merely what one might call a temporary arrangement for the homeless.... Here, barometers can no longer take any measure, compasses run wild. The people you encounter can do no one any harm; they are larvae in a life where the wind and sun might have existed, but there is almost no memory of these blessings.

The Enlightenment utopias shattered, like illusions, into a state of incompletion and into the tragic failure of the revolution of 1799. In perpetual mourning, the entrance to the Palazzo Serra di Cassano, opposite the Palazzo Reale, forever closed its doors that year, unable to continue looking out toward the house of kings who had betrayed their promises. The period of restoration began.

Urban Blocks and Individual Elements

During the first half of the nineteenth century, neoclassical architecture withdrew from the responsibilities for the overall design of a city, from urbanistic paternalism; it detached itself from the idea of the whole and instead produced *enclosures* within the existing city.

The neoclassical period in Naples, while brief in duration, produced a totality of architectural-planning situations that was both ambiguous and successful. There were elements from the eighteenth-century Enlightenment tradition, elements of bourgeois revolutionary utopia, elements of restoration that converged to form a language that, strangely, was both conformist and experimental, reductive and elegant, refined and abstract. It was a language that turned toward both past and future and, in any case, was projected in an international dimension. British models (Bath, London, and Edinburgh) had typologies of crescents, terraces, and squares, which produced an extraordinary homogenization of the urban fabric, with a direct effect on the connective residential fabric. In Russian models (St. Petersburg), the exceptional and princely character of the interventions achieved particular monumentality. And models of French derivation (the prototype being the Chaux saltworks by Claude-Nicolas Ledoux, with a subsequent example seen in Milan) had an organic integration between a system of exceptional interventions and a diffusion of high taste in residential building. But Naples had its own distinct characteristics. A system with "points and lines" developed that simply was inserted within areas of privilege but did not affect the general fabric of the city, which remained abandoned to a nameless fate. The refined and elegant language of large-scale public interventions (the botanical gardens, the astronomical observatory, the Villa Reale of Chiaia, the new cemetery) and large buildings (the San Carlo theater, the complex of the church of San Francesco di Paola and its colonnade) left a consistent but limited mark on the city.

The aristocratic residence withdrew into themes that were escapist, in search of an absolute, a sense of cultivation isolated from nature. It defended itself against a city that had become far too polluted and open, and exercised a "tragic" nostalgia for the past. Thus on the hills and outskirts, villas were built, the last privileged and exclusive refuges of an aristocracy that was nearing extinction: Villa Floridiana, Villa Lucia, Villa Acton, Villa Doria d'Angri.

But in reality, a moment had been reached when the aristocracy was becoming more bourgeois, indeed indistinguishable from the bourgeoisie, which, for its part, was seeking dignity. The alignment of the facades of the palaces along the new streets, such as the Riviera di Chiaia, built behind the Villa Reale, created a new organizing principle that evened out ancient, once insurmountable differences.

This was the end of a long history, and the city realized that it was changing forever. In the passage from the eighteenth to the nineteenth century, the city presented a double image. On the one hand, there were definitive representations intended for purely practical, administrative, and police-related purposes, based on scientific eighteenth-century cartography. The topographic lithographed maps by Luigi Marchese, dated 1840, depict the "city of Naples divided into twenty pieces," each of which corresponds to a quarter that is analyzed meticulously,

building by building, in terms of forms and functions. On the other hand, the city precincts had become too large to be perceived as a totality and had become a field in which a series of particular views could be discerned. The urban views of Edgar Papworth, dated 1835, unfold along an ideal path that leads from the eastern hill of Capodichino to the western one of Posillipo. In the drawings of Alfred Guesdon, the back-lit city shades off toward an indistinct horizon. Perhaps a city "panorama," in the original sense of the word as "overall view," could be grasped only as an accumulation of subjects (such as in a curious engraving dated 1840 in the Majello collection). Salvatore Fergola and Giacinto Gigante prefer to depict flashes of landscape and light, here and there within the city.

Naples had become a bourgeois city. During the nineteenth century its architecture became typologically repetitive and linguistically eclectic. There was an indifference to the diversity of styles, which were aligned and assembled together, like goods on counters at a market, where different pieces can be bought and combined, depending on the buyer's taste. City planning, however, wielded increasingly heavy tools of intervention: slum clearance, demolition, and expansion according to large-scale and uniform geometric themes.

The typology of the palace, now appropriated by the open-minded and productive bourgeois class, was enlarged to cover entire lots in the new urban scheme, the buildings opportunely strengthened by the use of iron and reinforced concrete. At the end of the century, the Rettifilo, Via Duomo, and Via Mezzocannone gutted the ancient Graeco-Roman center with broad sections of road, in imitation of the Parisian model. Along these streets, huge residential palaces and offices arose to hide, with their alignment of uniform facades, the ancient labyrinths. In the new quarters of Vasto and Vomero, enormous, regular buildings were laid out along streets that radiated out from new piazzas, modeled on Haussmann's Place de l'Étoile. An imposing landfill buried Monte Echia, the ancient acropolis of Parthenope, and created an artificial ground level on which the Santa Lucia quarter was developed, constructed for huge buildings that occupied entire blocks carved out by the streets. The neo-Renaissance style provided the greatest dignity and was appropriate to the severity of the new force that ruled government: financial power. This style provided an nonhierarchical code of "modern" (but not too modern) respectability.

The new century brought a great rupture in stylistic languages, which led to a radical rejection of traditions and a flowering of avant-garde movements in architecture and the arts.

The "palazzo" type, so profoundly linked to the city's classical culture, broke down. With the help of new skeletal structures, more easily expressed in iron and reinforced concrete, the original compact masonry building was replaced by neo-Gothic or Art Nouveau outer frames, and along the new, winding streets of the elegant, bourgeois residential quarter (Via Filangieri, Via dei Mille, Piazza Amedeo, Via del Parco Margherita), the last palaces were laid out along the sides of streets or the flanks of the hills, like a drapery, rippling and dispersing its architectural elements to ornament the street or landscape.

Palaces and villas

Typology

For a long period of time the Neapolitan palazzo, which arose and grew in an intimate, almost visceral relationship with its surroundings, was characterized more by its empty spaces—courtyards, gardens, entrance porches—than by its built volumes. The latter were by no means absent, and today, despite subsequent transformations, they still have great formal and stylistic merit. But there is no question that those residual "lungs" of air and light contain the initial matrix for the city's residential organisms. It is through these spaces that Naples breathes, amid the multitudinous echoes of those who live and work there, still safeguarding the city's innermost meaning.

Only the faintest vestiges remain of houses from the ancient Greek settlement. Built along the city's streets, but closed to the outside world, they were organized around interior courtyards. These sometimes had true peristyles, traces of which remain, dating back to the second century B.C., in the areas peripheral to central *Neapolis*, such as the zone around the first Policlinico or Piazza San Domenico Maggiore, where the Palazzo Corigliano now stands.

Moving forward in time, until the fourteenth century little or nothing of the city's medieval fabric could be seen, other than the chaotic layout of narrow streets intersecting the Corso Umberto or some residual building elements near the Via Marina. Boccaccio provides some descriptive hints, as he has the reader accompany Andreuccio of Perugia into the "district called Malpertugio." "Climbing the steps," the poet has us follow a beautiful woman, a fourteenth-century commoner, "into her hall... and from there... into her bedroom." Then, passing through "an exit" and "placing his foot upon a table," Andreuccio stumbles "into a narrow little street, as we often see between two houses, above two rafters, placed between one house and the other... all ugly, completely dirty.... But what lay beyond the closed walls, so near by, of the medieval houses, separated on one side by the narrow sewage ditch, open to the sky?

The space, the feel of the place, had to lie entirely within, on the other side of the walls, which had a few small openings to the outside. In the fifteenth and sixteenth centuries there were still elements consistent with this approach, with courtyards at regular intervals with rounded arcades on square stone piers, often covered in plaster. This is still seen in the Palazzo Filomarino and the Palazzo Carafa della Spina, on Via Benedetto Croce, or in the Palazzo Acquaviva d'Atri. The Palazzo Sanseverino, now the church of Gesù Nuovo, once had a splendid courtyard with stone piers and rounded arches. Arcades, now walled in, barely emerge through the plaster, like prehistoric fossils, designing an illusory two-dimensional space on the dirty walls and, in some instances, conveying the overall sense of the courtyard. Elsewhere the arcades double in height, becoming grand loggias, as in the Palazzo Casamassima, the Palazzo Filangieri di Arianello, and the courtyard at number 20 Via Nilo. These illustrate a tradition for which there are even older examples, such as the loggia interrupted by polygonal piers in the Palazzo Petrucci, built at the same time as Castelnuovo, in the Aragonese style. According to Roberto Pape, these solid stone piers were considered preferable to Tuscan columns on account of their much easier and more economical construction. They were often located in a corner or on one side of a courtyard, arranged in two, three, four, or more orders to "represent" the ascending rhythm of stairs. Such structures are visible, for example, in the Palazzo Casamassima or in the Palazzo Venezia.

In the first half of the eighteenth century, these alternating spaces and volumes developed into outright theatrical designs, with backdrops of green gardens and a play of stuccowork ornamenting the volumes and spaces. At this point the ancient models of open-air domestic tranquillity were replaced with a new style of ostentatious grandeur. While the palace facades were overwhelmed and not entirely visible in the narrow streets, there was an almost exclusive concentration on the ornate portals. But there were other facades within, fully developed in height and breadth, in the inner courtyards. There, the urban space, restricted in the small city streets, seemed to find an outlet through the entranceways, and was swallowed up inside the dwellings, in an indiscriminate mingling of public and private, spaces and persons. This is true in the two Palazzi di Sanfelice ai Vergini, as well as in numerous contemporary and subsequent imitations, up to buildings designed approximately a half century later by Pompeo Schiantarelli, on Via Foria, opposite the botanical gardens. These courtyards often opened up to the outside, behind and to the sides of the building, in the manner of certain monastery cloisters. Examples of this scheme are the seventeenth-century plan of the Palazzo Reale (first half of the century), with the "C"-shaped layout, open toward the sea, or the Villa Belvedere, on the Vomero hill. In another case, the sixteenth-century structure of the front courtyard of the Palazzo Casamassima, screened at the back by a three-arched loggia with the ground-floor arcades below, looked out over the sea until a second courtyard was built in the eighteenth century, by Ferdinando Sanfelice.

While the green of the surrounding landscape remained physically separate, it "entered" the palace in innumerable ways. In the opulent design by Domenico Antonio Vaccaro for the Palazzo Tarsia, the green areas, which no longer exist, were an integral part of the architecture. Sometimes the landscape entered the rooms in illusory fashion, in furnishings in the most private spaces, or through naturalistic paintings, as in the extensive collection that once furnished the rooms of the Villa Belvedere.

All this slowly changed around the turn of the eighteenth century, when the building typology became somewhat colder, expressing wherever possible a hierarchical relationship with the surrounding space, implicitly directed through the mechanisms of axial perspective, with a seemingly infinite view. Thus the Palazzo Doria d'Angri represents a theatrically composed "stage set," at the beginning of the Via Toledo, its tilted facade oriented to the widened street space in front. At right angles, an axis of alignment moves through the entrance vestibule, linking two courtyards and a pass-through space. This is in accordance with a principle analogous to the Caserta palace's "visual telescope" that connected the tree-lined avenue, a continuation of the "old Naples road," with the indefinite glimmer of the waterfall, crossing through the volume of the palace.

Early-nineteenth-century buildings, with their colonnades and pilasters, required space in order to be perceived. Thus the Villa Acton was stepped back from the Riviera di Chiaia, which, however, was sufficiently broad to accommodate numerous other neoclassical structures.

Around the mid-nineteenth century, the prevailing characteristic of interior open space vanished definitively, and with it, the very meaning of a historical relationship between palace and city. The facade of the bourgeois building block was an ephemeral and clumsy surface for displaying the decorum of the new ruling class, which found the most concrete reasons for its own legitimacy in the maximum exploitation of the built area.

Land and buildings assumed new values, no longer derived from the choice and ambitions of a single owner or the imagination of an architect. Suggestions of style or a taste for artisan touches or skilled labor were registered in a mechanical indifference to decorative details, which became interchangeable in the architectural layout of neo-Renaissance facades. Buildings and land became the terms of a new social dynamic. Numerous financial institutions came into being: "[T]o whom will land or apartment houses be sold, or money loaned for construction? Solely to partners in the 'Società Napoletana'; it is not necessary to put up much money to be a partner.... Houses... will not be built in a single area, but at various points throughout the city.... Furthermore, the Società has proposed that new houses be neither concentrated in a given area nor endowed with a working class or bourgeois character.... And if thus far we have described types of small houses, large ones can also be built. There will be a single system, only the decorations will be a bit more painstaking for the large residences." This is a brief passage from the program for one of the city's financial institutions, published in May 1885 in the *Bollettino del Collegio degli Ingegneri ed Architetti*. It explains why, at this point, courtyards and gardens—crucial elements of the city's urban space, and models and points of reference of environmental quality for centuries—were negated. In terms of architecture, the new prevailing concept of space valued cubic meters exclusively on the basis of property income. This approach transferred design to an urban dimension, mechanistically tying the quality of the architecture to urban location and to quantitative and dimensional terms, rather than to the characteristics of the clientele.

Palazzo Penne, Palazzo Diomede Carafa, and Palazzo Petrucci

The Palazzo Penne, overlooking the Largo San Demetrio, is one of the few examples of fifteenth-century residential architecture that preserves the original appearance of its principal facade. The windowless elevation has continuous rows of rectangular rustication, with a slightly protruding cornice on the upper part of the facade. Starting from the upper edge of the entrance, the first three rows of rustication have a feather motif at the center, the family arms and symbol of Antonio Penne, who was secretary and counselor to King Ladislao ("penna" means "feather"). The rows of rustication higher up are decorated at the center with the Anjou lily, a motif that continues up as far as the trefoil-arched coping on the corbels, which are decorated with crosses and crowns in honor of the king. The rustication probably is derived from Spanish influences, also present in Sicily (for example, in the Palazzo Steripinto di Sciacca), rather than from Tuscan culture.

According to Roberto Pane, the entrance design,

Palazzo Petrucci: the facade, originally two stories tall, defines the west side of Piazza San Domenico Maggiore.

Palazzo Penne, by R. D'Ambra, color lithograph, 1889.

following page
Palazzo Petrucci: detail of Renaissance entrance.

similar to that of the Palazzo Bonifacio, is a simplification of a pointed Gothic arch superimposed upon a depressed arch, also seen in the cloister of the Friars Minor of Santa Chiara and in the colonnade of the Incoronata. Examples of depressed arches that form a corner at the juncture of the side walls can be seen throughout the oldest parts of the city, and they continued to be common until the nineteenth century.

Here, the entrance arch is inscribed within a molded rectangle with the Penne coat of arms in the corners. On the curved edge, a late Gothic ribbon unfurls in relief, engraved with two verses by Martial: "QUI DUCIS VULTUS NEC ASPPICIS ISTA LIBENTER/OMNIBUS INVIDEAS IN—VIDE NEMO TIBI."

The cornice over the entrance bears the following inscription: "XX ANNO REGNO / REGIS LADISLAI / SUNT DOMUS HEC FACTE / NULLO SINT TURBINE FRACTE / MILLE FLUUNT MAGNI / BISTRES CENTUMQUATER ANNI." In other words, the building was erected in 1406 by Antonio Penne, descendant of Luca, a famous jurist. The family traces its roots back to the time of Robert of Anjou. Onofrio, who settled definitively in Naples, succeeded Antonio. The property later passed into the hands of the Rocca and then the Scannapieco family, who lived there in the mid-sixteenth century. Aloise Scannapieco gave the palazzo to his son, Giovanni Gerolamo Capano.

In 1662 creditors of the Capano family took over the property, and the ensuing dispute lasted until the penultimate decade of the century. In 1683 the Somascan order purchased it. During French rule, when religious orders were abolished, the Palazzo Penne was acquired and occupied by Abbot Teodoro Monticelli, who resided on the third floor and enhanced the spaces of the house with his rock collection and extensive library. The building has three floors and is built on a site that slopes down toward the sea, flanked by the Santa Barbara steps, which originally led to the beach. According to a detailed description written by Giuseppe Ceci in 1894, the first floor was surrounded "on the east side, with a majestic portico embellished with statues and a delightful garden planted with citrus trees and enlivened with fountains. The portico leads to four large rooms, their doors divided by a cross shape. They still have beautiful, if somewhat poorly preserved, tufa moldings. At the back, there was another apartment with various rooms, which looked onto another courtyard and a staircase, which led to an atrium—also embellished with fountains and a marble basin—which led to the Santa Barbara steps. One arrived at the second floor through the main courtyard, ascending a lovely open stone staircase that ended on a terrace surrounded by curved stone balconies, which in turn led to a large room and various apartments. The windows on the second floor look out over the Vicolo di Santa Barbara; they rest on the cornice at the top of the tall basement and look out, more or less, at the Palazzo Cuomo, a building we know was built more than fifty years later. Stone crosses span the windows, so that each is divided into four smaller openings, the upper two of which are square. Elegant moldings run all around, turning the frame into a protruding ribbon, resting on elegant little leaf-shaped brackets." Ceci continues, describing how "a ceiling with thick beams covered with large tiles protruded out from the gracious building, which had a single large room within. The next space was and still is the courtyard, which had to the left a wide stable, capable of accommodating sixteen horses, and its entrance, opposite the main body of the building."

The Palazzo di Diomede Carafa also preserves its original exterior, more or less intact. There is continuous rustication of tufa and gray stone elements, alternating in a sinuous pattern, with a look that is still medieval. The building must have been rebuilt on the site of a preexisting structure, since some medieval framework was discovered beneath the rustication. Furthermore, there is an epigraph that reads: "HAS COMES INSIGNIS DIOMEDES CONDIDIT AEDES & CARAFA/IN LAUDEM REGIS PATRIAEQUE DECORUM & EST ET FORTE LOCUS MAGIS APTUS ET AMPLIUS IN URBE & SIT SED AB AGNATIS DISCEDERE TURPE PUTAVIT."

On the other hand, the lack of an organic relationship between the building's various elements supports the hypothesis of reconstruction of a preexisting building owned by the same Carafa family. As Roberto Pane has noted, this seems to be indicated by the element in the left side of the courtyard, immediately after the porch: a fluted column with a capital taken from another site, which has a rechiseled ancient tombstone for a base. The column is surmounted by two flattened arches, one of which is supported, on the opposite side, by a capital similar to those in the arch of the porch. These elements, with the volume of the building above, are juxtaposed onto the older portico, made up of squat, octagonal stone piers and flattened arches. As in most cases with these structures, the inner surface of the arches echoes the appearance of the vertical supports. The piers and arches are similar to those in Castelnuovo, but while equally worked, they are always defined with cornices that make them formally autonomous from one another: for example, the way the upper arcade piers are separated from the upper facade wall of the courtyard.

The palazzo, to which a garden was also annexed—as

Sigismondo and Luigi Catalani recall—was filled with marbles and sculptures: statues, bas-reliefs, and funerary stones that ornamented the courtyard and staircase. There are still two busts to the right and left on the entrance cornice and a statue in a central niche. Against the rear wall inside the courtyard is a terracotta horse's head, a copy of an original by Donatello. On the exterior, below the cornice that crowns the palazzo, sculpted faces of Diomede Carafa and his wife adorn two corners of the building.

The central band of the complex trabeation of the marble entrance and the wooden doors are sculpted with the family's distinctive "signs," which also indicate commercial activities and economic power: a veritable "manifesto" that connoted their presence in the city.

The Palazzo Petrucci in Piazza San Domenico Maggiore has been compared to the Palazzo Diomede Carafa because of their similar entranceways. The Palazzo Petrucci probably dates to the fourteenth century, when Bertrando III of Balzo began the construction with "Gothic-style doors and windows." Hellen Rotolo includes this information, provided by Celano in the late seventeenth century, in her careful study, now being prepared for publication. Rotolo's preliminary examination of the scarce sources available on the building has enabled her to reconstruct the complex changes of ownership. Antonello Petrucci lived there in the second half of the fifteenth century. Born to a peasant family in Teano, he achieved a significant position in the Aragonese court and became one of the most powerful men under the reign of Ferrante I. He became tragically involved in a barons' conspiracy against the Aragonese dynasty, which came to a bloody end in Castel Nuovo.

Petrucci was succeeded by the D'Aquino family who lived there until 1698, when the building was sold to the governors of the Banco del SS. Salvatore. In her study, Rotolo notes that on this occasion, until the early eighteenth century, work on the interior was done to adapt the spaces for their new use, but without consistent exterior modifications. The ceiling ornaments on the first floor date to this period; they are characterized by simple decorative motifs, as well as a large canvas, which Rotolo has attributed to Antonio Dominici, on the basis of archival documentation. The painting depicts the *Triumph of Faith* and covers the entire ceiling of the reception hall on the second floor. This floor has access to a garden that is adjacent to the sacristy of the church of San Domenico Maggiore, which still preserves its seventeenth-century design, with a central hall and other spaces arranged along a curve. The garden, as Perrotta described it in 1828, was "planted with citrus trees, 234 spans long and 205 wide." It still contains the same type of vegetation. The entire green area is located on the first level, although much of it has been annexed by the apartment above. After the bank was shut down, the building passed into the hands of the state, in 1806, and became the audit office. Purchased in 1829 by Professor Giuseppe Galbiati, it was further renovated, both on the interior—returning it to its original function as a residence—and on the exterior, with a reconstruction of the facades and the addition of a third floor. This work was carried out by architect Giuseppe Califano, from 1829 to 1845.

Over time, numerous changes in ownership have annulled the building's original connotations, which, however, are still evoked through the flattened arches on the ground floor and the interrupted loggias on the two upper levels, where the faceted piers recall those of Castel Nuovo and the Palazzo Diomede Carafa.

Palazzo Petrucci: courtyard loggia.

Entrance to the Palazzo Carafa, by C. N. Sasso, in *Storia dei monumenti di Napoli*, 1856.

Palazzo Cuomo

Palazzo Cuomo, now the Museo Civico Filangieri, by R. D'Ambra, in *Napoli antica*, 1889.

The "Sala Agata," a reception hall named for Agata Moncada di Paternò, princess of Satriano.

The Palazzo Cuomo was built between 1404 and 1490. The Cuomo family has ancient roots, and we know that in 1292, Riccardo, lord of Albignano in Terra di Lavoro, an ancestor, was named by Charles II of Anjou to serve as vicar in Marseilles.

In 1451, Giovanni Cuomo purchased an adjacent house from Angelo Ferrajolo, "in pendino dictae ecclesiae Sancti Giorgii." He had a corner cupboard and interior staircase torn down and proceeded with the construction of the palazzo on the south side.

Angelo Cuomo, probably the son of Giovanni, continued with construction, engaging various Tuscan masters (Francesco di Filippo from Settignano, Ziattino di Benozzis from Settignano, Domenico Felice, and others), probably in accordance with a plan by Giuliano da Maiano.

The building was further expanded when Alfonso of Aragon, duke of Calabria (Leonardo, Angelo's son, was his equerry and secretary), purchased an adjacent piece of land from Francesco Scannasorice for five hundred ducats, which included a garden and house.

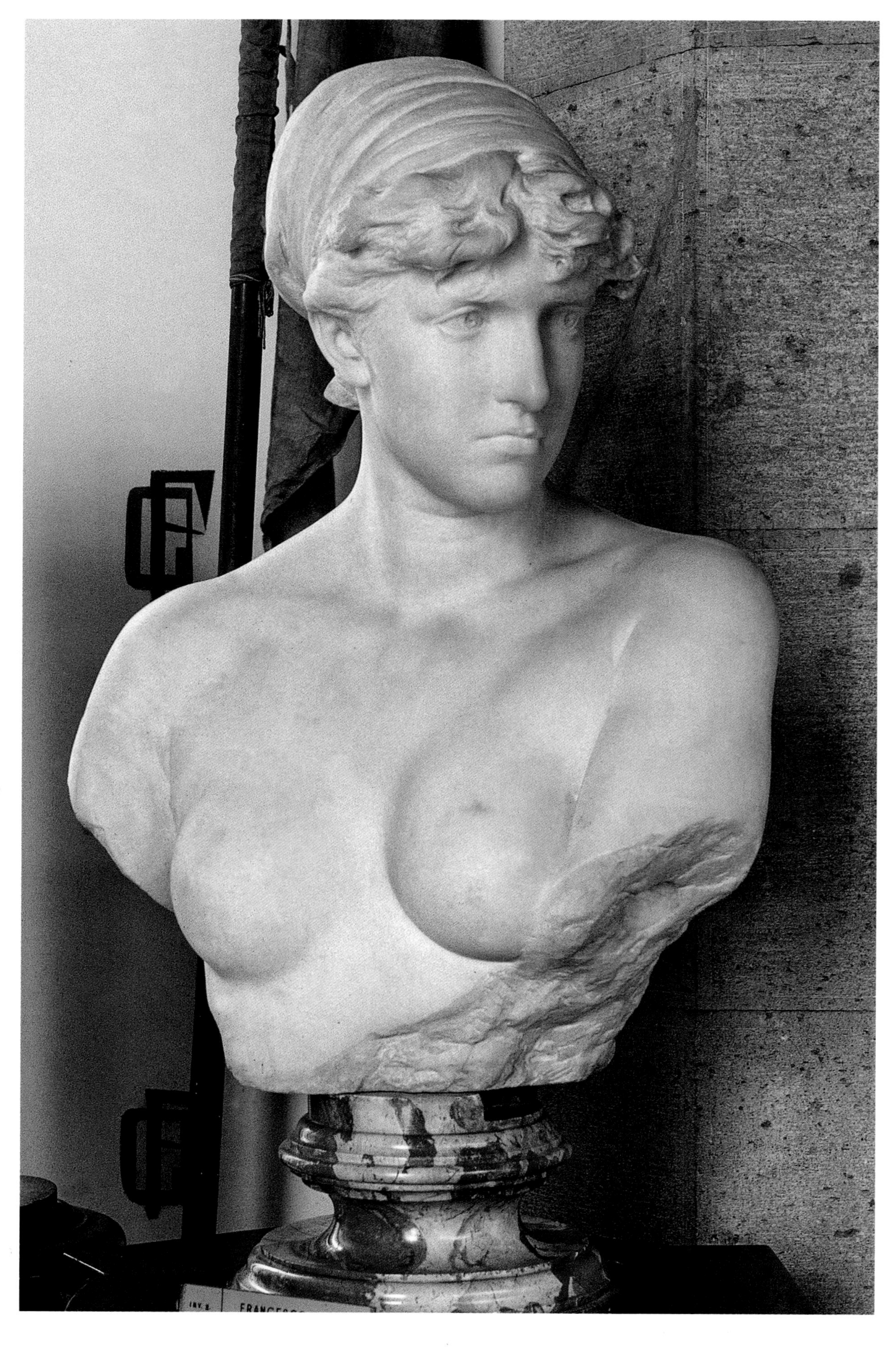

He gave it to Angelo, in order to allow him to complete his residence. The Cuomo family occupied the building until 1587, when the property was sold to the nearby monastery of San Severo Maggiore.

When laws were passed mandating the seizure of church property, the building was adapted for public offices. After the renovations were completed, a decision was made to widen the Via Duomo, and a long debate ensued about whether or not to tear down the building. In the end, it was "dismantled" and moved back about twenty meters. The iron roof trusses were made by Alfredo Cottrau's metalworks, located in Castellammare di Stabia.

After this work was completed, the building's function was in question. Don Gaetano Filangieri, prince of Satriano, offered to finance the renovation of the interior spaces, to house his extensive collection of art objects, some of which were inherited and some of which he had personally collected.

This was the genesis of the Museo Civico Gaetano Filangieri, established by royal decree on 16 August 1882 and endowed by Prince Filangieri with capital and an annual income. The museum opened on 8 November 1888.

The museum's collection includes paintings; medieval and Asian arms; majolica from Faenza, Gubbio, Castelli di Abruzzo, Casteldurante, and Cafaggiuolo; porcelain from Capodimonte

and elsewhere; crèche figures from the eighteenth and nineteenth centuries; ivories, inlaid woods, glasswork, tapestries and miniatures; marble busts, parchments, manuscripts, books; and finally coins and medals.

On account of the Second World War the museum was closed from 1941 to 1948 and reopened 29 September 1948. The two-storied building has three facades, each with a tall basement clad in stone, an intermediary zone of rough rustication corresponding to the first floor, and an upper portion with smooth rustication, surmounted by an overhanging, projecting cornice. The windows, with cross casings, are similar to those of the Palazzo Venezia in Rome. The wooden entrance door bears the Filangieri coat of arms.

The ground floor room is divided into three spaces covered by domed vaults, supported by four exposed stone arches set on eight piers placed against the walls. The floor has square stone paving. The surface of the vaults is covered in polychrome mosaic against a gold ground, with branches and leaves in arabesques, lotus flowers and sunflowers, interspersed with scrolls bearing the names of the most famous members of the Filangieri family. Five steps lead from the ground floor to the grand staircase, a rectangular spiral, which has forty monolithic stone steps. The walls around the staircase

preceding pages, left
Francesco Jerace, *Victa.*

preceding pages, right
B. Luini, *Madonna and Child*, 16th-17th century.

opposite
Ground-floor room divided into three bays, covered with domical vaults on stone arches.

below
One of the domical vaults on the ground floor.

2700
SECOLO XVI°
ERCOLE e L'IDRA

are decorated with the family coat of arms as well as marble and ceramic coats of arms from various eras.

On the floor above, to the left, is an openwork, walnut balustrade, fifteenth-century in style, with engraved, wrought-iron candleholders and rosettes.

Most of the upper floor is taken up by the "Sala Agata," named for Agata Moncada di Paternò, princess of Satriano and mother of the museum's founder. Preceded by a small portico made up of four inlaid walnut columns, the room is surrounded by a wide hanging walkway. The floor is covered in glazed tiles with coasts of arms, heraldic symbols and monograms of the Filangieri family. The tiles were produced at the Ceramics Workshop of the Industrial Arts Museum in Naples, created by the Filangieri Museum's founder. This room has two entrances with inlaid wooden columns. One entrance leads to an upper hanging walkway; the other leads to a room with glass cases containing the Filangieri family's formal diplomatic garments, as well as a series of Eastern and Asian arms. The hanging passage provides access to the library, two walls of which are paneled in walnut.

opposite
"Sala Agata," detail.

below
"Sala Agata," detail of the majolica pavement with coats of arms and symbols of the Filangieri family, made by the Ceramics Workshop of the Industrial Arts Museum of Naples.

Palazzo Venezia

The Palazzo Venezia, which is on Via Benedetto Croce, adjacent to the more famous Palazzo Filomarino, clearly dates back to the fourteenth century. We know that in 1412 King Ladislao of Durazzo gave the building, which was owned by the Sanseverino family of Matera, to the Venetian republic. From that time onward the building was called the Palazzo San Marco.

The area, part of the Nido district, was largely inhabited by the Brancaccio and Sanseverino families, who presumably lost the palazzo because of their loyalty to the French pretender, Louis II of Anjou. Louis, called by Joanna I of Anjou to oppose his nephew Charles III of Durazzo, entered Naples in 1381. Two years later, Joanna was assassinated. Ladislao of Durazzo succeeded Charles III in 1386 and remained on the throne until his death in 1414. At that time the building was considered "one of the most noble and most magnificent habitations," according to Gian Giacomo Corniani, ambassador from Venice, writing in 1706. Later, the absence of the

The "little Pompeiian house," added during the neoclassical period, in the interior garden.

following pages, left
Stucco medallion inside the "little Pompeiian house."

following pages, right
Interior of the "little Pompeiian house."

Venetian ambassador during the dispute between René of Anjou and Alfonso of Aragon enabled Amerigo Sanseverino, count of Capaccio, to once again occupy the property, which he claimed by right of inheritance. But in 1443 Alfonso approved and restored the gift of the house to the Republic of Venice and ordered Ferdinand of Aragon, duke of Calabria, his son and representative, to carry out his wishes.

The tradition of ambassadors in foreign localities was alien to the European states because of the dangers connected to intrigues that might threaten domestic rule. But the practice was in force in Italy and Germany, which were divided into many autonomous states, and it somewhat rapidly became general policy for other nations as well. During the fifteenth century, new forms of international relationships were increasingly characterized by permanence, stability, and continuity. In 1455 permanent embassies already existed in Milan, Florence, Venice, and Naples. This organizational system is the origin of the term "residente," what we would call an ambassador, for a diplomatic figure. This was the title held by the ambassador from Venice to Naples, beginning around 1565, when the Venetian republic also began to have permanent embassies in Milan and the Low Countries.

The Palazzo Venezia, at the time of its donation, was

half its current height, but still dominated the nearby Palazzo Brancaccio, later the Palazzo Filomarino. It was surrounded by broad gardens and orchards, which occupied part of the property belonging to the latter building, which must have been limited initially to the structure on the Via San Sebastiano. The original appearance of these buildings, like all civil buildings from the Angevin era, has now been lost. In any case, in the mid-fifteenth century the Palazzo Venezia became a true embassy, and it seems that it housed the Supreme Court during the third and forth decades of that century.

The use of the palazzo as an embassy, beginning in the second half of the fifteenth century, entailed the occupation of the second floor by the envoy and the ground floor by the consul. With the advent of Spanish rule in the early sixteenth century, the building was largely abandoned, leaving only the consul on the ground floor, with the western rooms probably set aside for service areas. But the Venetian senate was dissatisfied with this intermittent presence of ambassadors in Naples, and from 1565 to 1797 there was a permanent resident, with the addition, on certain occasions, of a special envoy. During Spanish rule, changes in the political balance followed the discovery of America and the opening of new commercial routes. The Venetian republic became less powerful, due to the Spanish presence in Lombardy and in southern Italy. Naples itself, part of the Spanish viceroyalty, became less important. As a result, the palace was neglected. By the early seventeenth century it was in terrible condition, and over the course of that century it underwent continuous repairs and restoration work. Significant figures were involved in this activity, such as Cosimo Fanzago and Bartolomeo Picchiatti, but the interventions neither distorted the building's simple lines nor led to new splendors.

From a survey conducted by architect Antonio Guidetti for Ambassador

Commemorative plaque in the garden.

opposite and next page
Frescoed decorations in the second-floor apartments.

SVRREXIT

Corniani, we learn that in 1706 the embassy's garden had "forty feet of citrus trees, oranges and lemons, and approximately one hundred feet of various trees bearing edible fruit."

Over time, the Venetian embassy took up less space, to the advantage of the adjacent Bisignano property, which was taken over by the Brancaccio family. In 1756 Prince della Rocca obtained an additional portion of the garden from the Venetian republic, in order to erect an arcade for his palazzo. Under the ownership of the Bisignano and later the Filomarino families, the garden areas were further reduced.

After the victory of the Austrians over Napoleon at Leipzig, in 1813, and the execution by firing squad of Joachim Murat two years later, the Treaty of Campoformio and then the Congress of Vienna led to the palace's annexation by Austria, which put it up for sale in 1816. The jurist Capone purchased the palazzo in the second decade of the nineteenth century; he transformed the back of the courtyard above the loggia, which had been filled with lemon and orange trees, cedars and vines. He had another building wing constructed, with a central facade stepped back in a sort of curved semicircle, with two rectilinear portions at the sides, open with two windows.

The loggia, with three arcades on the side at the back of the courtyard, was originally open but was closed off in 1686. Two windows were then opened in the tympanums of the side arches, and were later enlarged. The original stone balustrade was replaced in the nineteenth century by an iron railing. The staircase on the left must have been built and enlarged during the seventeenth century. In fact, at the beginning of the eighteenth century, reliefs by Antonio Guidetti show that the building had reached its current dimensions.

The interior no longer has the pictorial decorations that must once have been present. The building, which has three stories above the ground floor and mezzanine level, has a simple, severe, arched entrance. A segmented arch leads from the entrance hall to the courtyard. On the left is an open stairway with three supporting arches, with the widest arch at the center, with iron handrails (added later) and an iron and glass roof, probably from the early twentieth century. The height of the building element on Via Benedetto Croce is repeated on the two continuous sides of the courtyard, with a crowning element of small suspended arches. There is a partial attic. The portion of the building contiguous to the staircase was later raised up, aligning it with the rest of the structure.

New interventions, with the insertion of commercial shops inside the courtyard, have involved further modifications.

At the back, in front of the so-called "little Pompeiian house"—which has a facade with three bays separated by pairs of Doric columns and surmounted by a triangular pediment—are flower beds with tall plants, a reminder of a now vanished environment. Even if little of the Palazzo Venezia's original configuration remains, the building is still quite significant because it provides evidence of a universe of political and economic relationships at the height of the Renaissance, when the Venetian republic and the city of Naples played leading roles in the world.

Palazzo Filomarino

Entrance by Ferdinando Sanfelice, overlooking Via Spaccanapoli.

Artisans' workshops in the courtyard portico.

The site where the Palazzo Filomarino currently stands was already occupied at the beginning of the fifteenth century by the "hospicium Joannelli Branchacii dicti Guallarella," or the house of the Brancaccio family, represented by a person known as "Guallerella," or "the hernia-sufferer." This information is taken from a document transferring the palazzo from King Ladislao to the Venetian republic, dated 15 August, 1412. Traces of pointed arches from the fourteenth century have been found in the wall of the grand staircase. Otherwise, the early construction, according to Benedetto Croce, "probably [consisted of] the sole wing that presently overlooks the Via San Sebastiano." The rest was occupied by the gardens and courtyards of the Palazzo Venezia, described as "quoddam hospicium magnum, cum curti et jerdeno, salis, cameris et diversis aliis membris inferioribus et superioribus" in a document of the time as reported by Croce. The adjacent palace was used, although not uninterruptedly, by the Venetian republic for its embassy in Naples. The somewhat

preceding page
Painted canvas of the central coffer in the ceiling of a room on the *piano nobile*, now a lecture hall for the Italian Institute for Historical Studies.

Benedetto Croce's library: the "red room," overlooking Via San Sebastiano, furnished by Benedetto Croce with Russian furniture, after the palace was plundered by the Fascist regime during the 1930s.

extended periods of partial abandonment undoubtedly encouraged plans to expand the building, which originally belonged to the Brancaccio family, and which passed into the hands of the Sanseverino di Bisignano family in the early sixteenth century.

In fact, information exists that in 1511 Prince Bernardino Sanseverino di Bisignano, having returned from exile in France in 1507, decided to expand and rebuild the palazzo. He approached the Venetian republic about taking over a piece of land belonging to the adjacent Palazzo Venezia. Initially he was granted a lease in perpetuity, but only a few days later the property in question was definitively given over to him.

According to Dominici, whose opinion is corroborated by later scholars, the additions to the building were the work of the sixteenth-century Neapolitan architect known as Mormando. In 1647 the building was damaged during riots by the populace. From the nearby bell tower of Santa Chiara, the Spaniards bombarded the building, in which the Neapolitans were hiding.

After the death of Prince Nicola Bernardino, in 1606, which provoked a series of inheritance disputes, the building was acquired by the Filomarino della Rocca family, which sought to further expand the structure over the course of the seventeenth century. A letter from the Venetian ambassador, Pietro Dolce, dated 1 July 1642, relates that the della Rocca family had requested a piece of land adjacent to the Palazzo Venezia. The request was turned down, and some years later Pietro Dolce took over the restoration work of the embassy. According to Croce, the Filomarino della Rocca family subsequently obtained, in 1756, "a piece of the garden to erect the archway of their palazzo." According to Gino Doria, the rooms of the della Rocca palazzo were furnished with many paintings by the most important artists of the time, as well as a collection of fourteenth-century portraits of men and women, and frames and various "ornaments." Giambattista Vico, the young princes' schoolmaster, was a frequent visitor.

One of the building's most significant architectural elements is the portico. As Roberto Pane has observed, in Naples stone porticos with arcades open on four sides were characteristic only of cloisters and a few examples of civil architecture, such as, in addition to the Palazzo Filomarino, the Palazzi Gravina and Caracciolo d'Oppido. According to Pane, the replacement of Tuscan-style columns with stone piers "can be attributed, not so much to an evolution in taste, but rather to the greater ease and economy in building a column with superimposed blocks of stone rather than a monolithic shaft of marble." The

One of the reading rooms in Benedetto Croce's library.

entrance is another significant element, and Luigi Catalani has noted that "in the early eighteenth century it was rebuilt according to the architecture of knight Ferdinando Sanfelice, who removed part of the window-sill cornice, which he then adapted to balconies."

The founding of the Institute of Historical Studies dates to the beginning of the twentieth century and is a result of the arrival of Benedetto Croce, who acquired and moved into the third floor of the palazzo.

A corner room of Benedetto Croce's library, looking out over Spaccanapoli and Via San Sebastiano.

Detail of the pictorial decoration of the canvas on the ceiling of a room on the *piano nobile*, now the office of the director of the Italian Institute for Historical Studies.

Palazzo Marigliano

The Palazzo di Capua dates back to the early sixteenth century and was completed in 1513. It became known as the Palazzo Marigliano during the first half of the nineteenth century, when the count of Saponara—into whose possession the building passed when the di Capua family died out in 1792—sold it to Don Saverio Marigliano, a civil court judge.

On the basis of rare archival documents and an in-depth stylistic analysis, the building can be attributed to Giovanni Donadio, known as Mormanno or Mormando, the most important architectural personality in Naples in the early sixteenth century. Historian Bartolomeo Capasso has located a document that describes the architect as a "Neapolitan citizen, organist, and most excellent architect, who worked throughout this city, in service to the royal court, as well as to the churches, barons, gentlemen, and other citizens of the city." The artist, originally from Calabria, also devoted himself to making organs, and documents give evidence of this activity in the late fifteenth century. Cured after a long illness so severe that he had made out his will, he also took up architecture. His first work was the construction of his own house on Via San Gregorio Armeno, where the atrium and staircase still show the signs of Tuscan influence.

During those same years, Giuliano da Maiano, Francesco di Giorgio, and other Tuscan artists were present in Naples, and the work of Mormando is always compared to that of Giuliano da Maiano, with Pietro Summonte stressing how Mormando "imitated ancient things." The stylistic analogies that relate Mormando to the Tuscan school can be seen, in particular, in the facade of the church of Santa Maria della

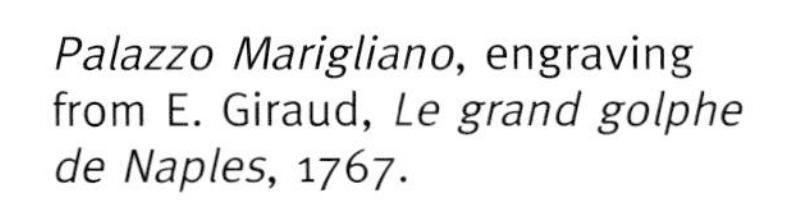

Palazzo Marigliano, engraving from E. Giraud, *Le grand golphe de Naples*, 1767.

Staircase entrance, detail decorated with the family motto.

following pages
Majolica pavement, made in Naples in the 19th century.

Stella, known as Santa Maria "delle Paperelle." Mormando would have been exposed to the style of Giuliano da Maiano and Bramante through nearby architectural achievements in Rome. Summonte, in the same letter as quoted above, also relates how the artist, "because of the lack of comfort in the place, forced by the scarcity of terrain, was unable to express his brilliant ideas. . . ."

In fact, due to lack of space and the narrowness of the street, the facade design of the Palazzo di Capua, the most important work attributed to Mormando, reflects conditions that constantly required a focus on elements that could be admired most easily from close up. Thus the elevation is characterized by a contrast between the marble and stone moldings and by attention to details in the lower portion of the facade. The facade is distinguished by the composite style of the capitals on the fluted pilasters. Meanwhile, the upper level is punctuated by smooth pilasters with more modest Corinthian capitals. The lower portion of the facade encompasses two stories spanned by fluted pilasters resting on a continuous base, with a lower cornice where the building meets the ground and an upper cornice supporting the vertical relief elements. The third level has rectangular windows, each surrounded by a broad and refined frame with a window sill balanced by an overhanging rectilinear coping above; smooth pilasters with Corinthian capitals punctuate the wall surface at regular intervals. The upper band bears the motto "MEMINI." Roberto Pane, like Mario Rotili before him, has noted that "a thin band, formed by a molding and lintel, is delineated along the pilasters, architrave, and base, outlining the entire interior rectangle. This accentuates the rectangle's boundary and provides a gradual passage, preventing the projecting structure from appearing too abrupt." As Pane has also noted, this element is typical of Mormando's style; it is seen in the Palazzo Corigliano and again in two works of this type by Gianfranco di Palma—the Palazzo del Panormita and the wide elevation of the church of Santi Severino e Sossio. In this way, there is an overall balance, with individual architectural elements resolved in a decorative and pictorial key. Unfortunately, beneath the square windows of the lower level, the tall, continuous base was interrupted in the nineteenth century by the opening of spaces to accommodate commercial shops, and the balanced facade was heavily violated by the addition of another level, covered by a double-hipped roof.

Many noble palazzi were built along *decumanus* in the early sixteenth century. These included, in addition to the Palazzo di Capua, the Palazzo Carafa della Spina, the Palazzo Carafa di Montorio, the Palazzo Diomede Carafa, the Palazzo Acquaviva d'Atri and others, all in the Nido district. Indeed, there must have been a precise relationship between the siting of these noble dwellings and the presence of the respective families in a particular area of the city, in that the placement of a palazzo was tied to issues of prestige and proof of nobility. Each district had a *sedile*, a small building with a square plan and domed roof, in which the nobility's elected representatives would meet, to which representatives of the people were later added. This institution dates back to 1268 and has direct precedents in the *regiones* of the ducal period and the *tocchi* of the Swabian era.

Many palaces, including those along the Via San Biagio dei Librai, are derived from the transformation of the layout of the early court houses, where the open interior spaces and gardens compensated for the lack of space and light in the narrow streets. In the Palazzo di Capua (later Marigliano), the courtyard and door to the garden had considerable importance, for they gave a perspective of space and light to the back of the building. Beyond the entrance hall, one entered the courtyard, the appearance of which is the result of alterations carried out beginning in 1745 by Bartolomeo di Capua, prince of Riccia, who entrusted the work to the royal court engineer, Matteo Bottiglieri. During this work, a raised narrow passage was built that extended the entrance hall, and the eastern portion of the building was expanded. The courtyard was shortened and, later the three-flight staircase, previously located in a protected position to the right, was moved to the end of the courtyard, giving a scenographic conclusion to the open space. Previously the garden must have been more extensive and arranged on two levels, as seen in a historical map of the city. It must have remained thus throughout the entire eighteenth century, accessible from the *piano nobile* of the palazzo (rather than from the courtyard), through a loggia that led to a raised floor, which in turn led, via a staircase with many flights, to a still existing hanging garden.

The courtyard to the left, after the entrance hall, leads to the main staircase, through a splendid marble entrance with vertical bands that create a double molding, the inner one smaller, with a bean motif, the other one with a "lion's paw" motif. The molding does not extend all the way to the ground but rests on bases adorned with arms and cuirasses in relief. Here too, the motto "*memini*" appears on the band beneath the strongly projecting horizontal coping.

On the second *piano nobile* of the building, a covered staircase with ribbed vaults and a tall stone skirting leads

to the government archive office for Campania. The present condition of the interior furnishings makes it impossible to deduce their original state. Nevertheless, various elements remain that date back to the eighteenth and nineteenth centuries. In the first space, paved in square black and white tiles from the nineteenth century, two oval paintings by Giovan Battista Maffei, one above the other, depict allegorical scenes. Dated 1765, these have rococo frames in green lacquered wood, designed by the engineer Felice Bottiglieri. According to Diodato Colonnesi, these panels were part of the old palazzo's "room of mirrors." The doors appear to be from the seventeenth century.

In the Hall of Armor,

Apartment on the *piano nobile*, now the Archives Office, oval ornamental panel, late 18th century, above the right door in the east wall of the *salone delle feste*, or drawing room, now a conference hall. This is one of a series of seven ornamental panels in neoclassical style, each depicting a floral still-life with putti, framed by gilded wood inlay work against a white ground.

Apartment on the *piano nobile*, now the archives office, oval ornamental panel, above the north door of the entrance hall, from the *boiserie* of the "room of mirrors," painted in *grisaille* by Giovan Battista Maffei, a figurative and ornamental painter. The panel depicts an allegorical scene, probably *Vanity*. The carved and gilded frame in green lacquered wood is in pure rococo style; it was made by A. Bozzaotra, a master carver and by G. De Luca, a master gilder, from a design by architect Felice Bottiglieri.

which has a high ceiling in dark wood, the walls are outlined, high up, by a series of coats of arms of noble Neapolitan families related to the Marigliano family. Another room, this too with a wooden ceiling, leads to the great reception hall, the interior and exterior openings of which are surmounted by oval shapes containing still-life paintings, flanked by two figures of children and other images with white frames and gilded carving in neoclassical style.

The tile floor, part of which was installed in 1746, was created by Giuseppe Massa. The ceiling still has part of a fresco executed by Francesco de Mura, to commemorate Bartolomeo di Capua's saving of Charles III Bourbon in 1744, during the battle of Velletri. The fresco was largely destroyed by wartime bombings and restored by the Marigliano family.

A private chapel, with a tile floor with a large band of faux green, white, and black marble, contains a mural painting by Giovan Battista Maffei.

The staircase at the back of the courtyard, which has eighteenth-century iron balustrades between stone piers, leads to a raised tiled terrace, built by Giuseppe Massa in 1747. This leads to the printing house offices. Among the plants in the garden there is a beautiful fountain, executed in 1740 by the marble-worker Carlo d'Adamo.

Detail of the vestiges of paving, a mixture of fired brick and enameled tiles, in the drawing room, the present-day conference hall. These were made in 1746 in the ceramics workshop of Giuseppe Massa and have a recurring heraldic theme, a dove flying over the mountains.

Palazzo Casamassima

The 16th-century loggia at the back of the first courtyard, with an arcade above, initially opened toward the garden, but later it was integrated into Ferdinando Sanfelice's design, with the creation of a second courtyard in the early 18th century.

The balustrade of the first-floor arcades, looking toward the first courtyard.

The Palazzo Casamassima, one of the remaining noble sixteenth-century palaces, is located at 8 Via Banchi Nuovi. The building stands at the boundary between the old *Neapolis* and the medieval expansion into an area characterized by numerous significant residences. One of these, the palazzo of Alfonso Sanchez, marchese of Grottola, still has traces of sixteenth-century Tuscan influence. The palazzo of the abbot of San Giovanni Maggiore was occupied in the mid-sixteenth century by Tommaso Cambi, a Florentine banker. The latter building overlooks Piazza San Giovanni Maggiore, while along Vico San Geronimo there is another entrance and a series of small sixteenth-century windows on the second floor. One of its rooms was frescoed by Giorgio Vasari, and these paintings were still present in the nineteenth century, three hundred years later.

The Palazzo Casamassima was built during the last decade of the sixteenth century. In October 1569 an extremely violent flood destroyed many buildings in the area and resulted in the creation of a small square

where merchants sold their wares. The building faced onto this space, and its side facade incorporated the earlier building's staircase, which opened into the first courtyard. The present three-story facade has shops on the ground floor, a first row of windows that extend no higher than the majestic and severe arched entrance, a second row of larger windows and a final row of openings below the cornice. The openings, originally windows, were later transformed into balconies, in keeping with local tradition.

The scale and decoration of the entrance compared to the facade's other elements are the result of the impossibility of seeing the facade as a whole from an adequate distance, due to the narrowness of the street. The entrance hall, covered with a barrel vault, leads to a rectangular courtyard, the left corner of which opens onto a rare example of an open sixteenth-century staircase with double arches separated by a pier. The back wall is closed off by a loggia with three rows of superimposed arches, beyond which there was a garden.

Fresco by Giacomo del Po, illustrating the story of *Cupid and Psyche*, on the ceiling of one of the rooms in the gallery, looking out over the second courtyard, on the second *piano nobile*.

Ground-floor courtyards characterized by continuous arcades on stone piers were not infrequent in Naples, where, for economic reasons, Tuscan-style columns were not often used. This type of courtyard can be seen in the Palazzo Orsini Gravina, which now houses the School of Architecture of the University of Naples, and in the Palazzo Bisignano, later called Palazzo Filomarino. The Palazzo Sanseverino, now the church of Gesù Nuovo, also must have had this type of courtyard.

The layout of the Palazzo Casamassima, analogous to many contemporary and nearby buildings in the style of Giovan Francesco di Palma, took advantage of the geography of the site which sloped down behind the building, thus allowing a view of the sea beyond the garden. The garden was designed by Antonio Nigrone, "fountain maker and water engineer," who created fountains with kiosks and loggias decorated with naturalistic motifs and an array of water diversions.

This decorative legacy is now completely lost, but the great Neapolitan dwellings can be compared to the most important residences in Rome, in terms of sixteenth- and seventeenth-century style. A review of the history of Palazzo Casamassima's construction shows that it began during a period of strong residential and social expansion, when a great deal of land was annexed by the nobility, occupying every free space in the city and resulting in frequent disputes. It is no accident that the new emerging class was a professional bourgeoisie composed largely of lawyers. The building, created for the Orsini di Gravina family, belonged to Lelio Orsini; in 1631, it passed into the hands of a cousin, Pietro Orsini, prince of Solofra. After renting the palazzo to Matthias Tijstheuschi, the Polish papal envoy, he sold it in 1633 to the extremely wealthy Giulia Gonzaga dei Conti di Novellara, wife of the Spaniard Francesco de Campo. In 1637 the building was taken over by the Somascan priests of the nearby church of San Demetrio. In 1658 they were forced to sell it to Antonio de Ponte, a representative of the new emerging class of professionals and entrepreneurs.

From 1707 to 1716 the palazzo underwent important alterations, entrusted to Ferdinando Sanfelice, who worked on the loggia, the paintings, and the inlay work of the gallery alcove. Sanfelice created a new courtyard beyond the loggia, with two side elements and a closed side that, in a certain way, echoed the theatrical style of the late Baroque period. The garden was sacrificed to the need for expansion, and the loggia assumed the same dramatic and perspectival function as the famous open staircases in numerous projects by the same architect. Sanfelice, who would also build the Palazzo Melofioccolo, behind the Palazzo Casamassima, was representative of a new class of architects and artisans who had a strong entrepreneurial spirit and whose work defined the style of the first half of the eighteenth century.

On the second *piano nobile*, in the rooms overlooking the second courtyard, the architect created a gallery, originally open to the loggia and now illuminated by only two balconies. These were probably the most elegant spaces in the building. The only remnant is the fresco by Giacomo del Po, illustrating the story of *Cupid and Psyche*, which was intended as a reference to the moral qualities of the owner. The two far ends of the room have depictions of Cupid as a child and Cupid as an adult; Psyche is portrayed between them, at the center, on a chariot in the sky, receiving the gift of eternity.

This sort of decoration was very common in Neapolitan residences during Austrian rule. There was a tendency to use the work of art and, more generally, the decorative scheme, for celebratory purposes, closely tied to the wishes of the owners. Giacomo del Po was the most important exponent of this style, which, in its emphasis on delicate and precious colors, becomes increasingly decorative in form and free from representational content.

Cupid and Psyche, detail.

Palazzo Cellammare

Arch by Ferdinando Fuga on the entrance ramp.

opposite and following pages
Detail from G. van Wittel, *Il borgo di Chiaia da Pizzofalcone*, early 18th century (Naples, collection Banco di Napoli).

Palazzo Cellammare, once the property of the abbot of Stigliano, was built in the first decades of the sixteenth century. We can only deduce its original overall appearance from old views of the city, which show a building of significant size, near the city walls, in an essentially agricultural setting. The next owner, Luigi Carafa di Stigliano, took over the property in 1531. He decided to completely renovate the building, which, under the presumable guidance of architect Ferdinando Manlio, assumed a turreted appearance similar to that of the Palazzo Reale Vecchio or Castel Capuano. This was also a typical style for many residences along the coast and in the interior, documented in a sixteenth-century representation of the populous Sanità district, which developed in the hinterland north of the city and was dense with crenellated structures.

Thus the cinquecento appearance of the palazzo was defined by an exterior courtyard with a sloping tower at one corner. A broad entryway surmounted by an arch leads to an interior courtyard, which preserves

View of the palazzo from above, seen in its present urban context.

Palazzo Cellammare, from Via Chiaia.

the original layout in the rectangular openings along the perimeter with square stone cornices on the ground level and around the windows on the upper floors. In one corner is an entrance to a sixteenth-century staircase, the steps of which were originally in stone, with flying buttresses punctuated by arches and stone piers.

In 1689, when the last prince of Stigliano, Nicola Guzman Carafa, died, the building was seized for taxes and was then purchased in 1700 by Antonio Giudice, prince of Cellammare and duke of Giovinazzo. The new proprietor undertook radical renovations. He had already taken possession of the palazzo in 1696, when the viceroy, the duke of Medinacoeli, was housed there.

The most elegant and typical architectural dwellings were sometimes used as settings for particular events or to house import-ant personalities, or even as temporary residences for the viceroys. The Giudice family was very close to the duke of Medinacoeli, viceroy in Naples from 1695 to 1702, and remained loyal to the duke even after the arrival of the Austrians. The prince of Cellammare followed Philip V Bourbon in the war of Lombardy and, in 1707, followed the Spanish viceroy who withdrew to Gaeta. That same year he was imprisoned in Naples, first in Castel Sant'Elmo, then in Castel dell'Ovo, from which he was freed in 1715. These events inevitably left their mark on the history of the palazzo.

Prior to the purchase of the palazzo by the prince of Cellammare, work was done by architect Francesco Antonio Picchiatti, between 1668 and 1670. The staircase of the palazzo is particularly interesting, not only in and of itself, but also because it is contemporary with and perhaps similar to the one built in the Palazzo Reale by the same architect in 1651 but later demolished. Another significant figure is Giovan Battista Manni, who designed the monumental staircase that is located through the entryway built by Ferdinando Sanfelice in the early years of the eighteenth century.

After the death of Manni (1728), Giovan Battista Nauclerio became involved, working on the chapel dedicated to the Virgin of Carmelo, from 1727 to 1729. But even while Nauclerio was actively engaged, many aspects of the building can be linked to Ferdinando Fuga, who was surely present at the site in 1729. All the elements—the entrance, the interior rhythm of the piers, the cornices and the quatre-foil recess of the vaults, the illusionistic women's gallery beneath a faux sky—contribute to create a spatial volume that expresses a felicitous marriage between the architectural tradition of the Roman school and a Neapolitan taste for the dramatic.

The rustication of the sloping base of the palazzo and the entrance arch can also be attributed to Fuga; these were created during renovation work that took place after the departure of Antonio Giudice, in 1726. The arch is connected to the Neapolitan Baroque tradition, seen in entrances such as the one by Cosimo Fanzago in the Palazzo Maddaloni. It anticipates some of Fuga's later solutions.

In the overall design of the palazzo, the gardens, which date to the first half of the sixteenth century, assume great importance. During that period, many parks and cultivated areas were laid out, particularly in newly developed urban areas. This was a transitional moment for dwellings that fell into a category somewhere between suburban villa and city residence. Since the

Corner of the palazzo from the main entrance.

Exterior staircase.

cinquecento, the gardens of the Palazzo Cellammare have been organized on two levels. Ferdinando Manlio followed the general layout, and Giovanni da Nola created the fountain for the "padiglione" (pavilion) in the "strada di mezzo" (central street), only some traces of which remain today.

Between 1760 and 1782 Michele Imperiali, who occupied the palazzo as a tenant, made many transformations. During this period, two gardens behind the palazzo were extended up the Mortelle hill, and a third was developed in the direction of the palazzo of the marchese del Vasto.

During the last twenty years of the nineteenth century, the upper gardens were eliminated. Subsequent construction and urban planning projects to complete the "western quarter" by the end of the century also further limited but did not completely annul the theatrical vision that exploited the slope of the terrain to provide visual perspectives, emphasizing the wealth and power of the owner.

Detail of the windows.

The rear garden.

Palazzo Sangro di Sansevero and the Sansevero Chapel

Entrance vestibule.

Like many other buildings in the area, the Palazzo Sansevero was built in the sixteenth century, at the behest of the prince of Sansevero, Don Paolo de' Sangro. According to Luigi Catalani, the design for the building was by Giovanni da Nola. Information exists about renovation work, which took place at the same time as the construction of the chapel in 1593, under the supervision of Gianfrancesco de' Sangro. Work on both the palazzo and the chapel continued until 1642. From this date onward, there is no information about further construction until 1744, when Raimondo de' Sangro resumed work. The building has sober lines, perhaps in part because the narrowness of the street did not allow the facade to be appreciated as a whole. The marble and stone entrance is particularly noteworthy, with an archway in the middle, between two half-columns with horizontal bands, organically linked by the adjacent edging that frames the entire area up to the level of the overhanging balcony. The tympanum, with its sumptuous projecting cornices, is interrupted at the center by

P. Petrini, *Palazzo Sansevero*, engraving on copper, 1718.

l Palazzo del Principe di S. Seuiero Sangro
ono due galerie ben dipinte con uaghe logge all' intorno

the magnificent family coat of arms. The latter is attributed to Vitale Finelli, who is thought to have executed it in 1621 according to a design by Bartolomeo Picchiatti.

We know that from the middle of the subsequent century Raimondo de' Sangro renovated the building, one of many projects he was working on, including the royal chapel. Before his death, de' Sangro had completed only the facade and, according to Catalani, the renovation of the entrance. At that time, the building was embellished with decorative works and paintings. The stucco bas-reliefs in the entrance atrium depict *Bacchanals*, compositions formerly assigned by Catalani to Giuseppe Sanmartino; their design was later attributed to Francesco Celebrano and the actual execution to Gerardo Solferino. Francesco Celebrano is also responsible for the two surviving ceiling frescoes on the mezzanine of the palazzo, *Allegory of Summer* and *Allegory of Winter*, executed after 1766. Here the artist, who was known for works in marble, wood, and polychromed terracotta, reveals considerable pictorial talents, and his work displays a rococo luminosity and lively sense of color. In 1889 the left wing of the building collapsed, destroying frescoes by Belisario Corenzio that commemorated family exploits. These three rooms on the *piano nobile* constituted the "apartment of the patriarch," according to a note by the marquis de Sade in his *Voyage en Italie* (1766).

During the eighteenth century the palazzo experienced its period of greatest splendor, particularly with Raimondo de' Sangro, who connected it to the rebuilt chapel through a raised passageway, which later collapsed. The interior spaces were filled with all sorts of strange and marvelous objects, made by the prince himself or the results of experiments carried out with stones and minerals. According to the aforementioned note, "the little apartment on the second floor of the palazzo, where the prince stays, ... contains the following things invented by him: a painting of his daughter Erodiade, ... composed of wool of various colors, which, seen in profile against the light, looks like a sort of wool velvet; halftones of this figure are so well shaded, that it is the equal of any other painting in oil. ... A case with different levels contains an arrangement of ninety-six squares of white Carrara marble, each painted a different color. Most of these

Neapolitan school, early 18th century, in the style of Paolo De Matteis, *Triumph of Galatea*.

so skillfully imitate actual types of stone that they cannot be distinguished from the real thing. ... The remaining ones are imaginary, in very faint colors outside the natural order. The paint enters the marble, penetrating it layer by layer . . . so that if it is cut into more stones, they are colored already. ... The most beautiful invention of the Prince ... is that after the Carrara marble has been painted, it acquires the same hardness as Eastern marbles." The marquis continues: "True paintings of white marble can be seen, painted with beautiful figures in different types of red. ... Another wonderful invention by the prince is the counterfeiting of lapis lazuli, at very little expense, which no professor can distinguish from the real thing, after it has been sawed into thin slices." These observations give an idea of what the atmosphere must have been within the palazzo during the second half of the century of the Enlightenment, amid the myriad examples of an artificial reality, recreated in a laboratory, perhaps an expression of a need for aristocratic escape from the demands of everyday life.

Rosanna Cioffi has written that in 1898, with the death of Michele II, the last direct descendant of the family, the property began to be dismantled. An English woman, Elisa Graghan, was named as one of Michele de' Sangro's heirs. After

Allegory of Spring, fresco by Francesco Celebrano, 18th century.

following page
Allegory of Spring, fresco by Francesco Celebrano, detail.

numerous disputes, she was assigned the wing of the palazzo that contains Celebrano's frescoes. However, she lived in Paris and rented the property to an order of cloistered nuns, who covered over the frescoes, by lowering the ceiling in the room. In 1933 the apartment was acquired by Knight Commander Antonio Morano, who rediscovered the painted ceilings and finally brought them to light. The room currently houses the venerable Morano publishing house.

During the last decade of the sixteenth century, Gianfrancesco de' Sangro began construction of the Sansevero family chapel. According to tradition, the site had been occupied previously by a garden enclosed by a wall painted with an image of the Madonna holding the body of the dead Christ. This *Pietà* was seen by chance by a man who was being taken to prison. Later, when he was found innocent, he expressed his gratitude by placing a silver lamp at the site so that the sacred image could be constantly illuminated. Gianfrancesco de' Sangro himself fell seriously ill and was healed after praying to the *Pietà* painted on the wall, which led him to build the first small chapel, in 1590.

In 1608, Alessandro, patriarch of Alexandria and son of Gianfrancesco Paolo, prince of Sansevero, expanded the first chapel so that it could house the remains of family members. Alessandro later rejected the title of second prince of Sansevero, in favor of his brother Paolo. Work on the chapel was interrupted in 1642, at which time the renovations of the nearby palazzo were also brought to a halt.

In 1744 Raimondo de' Sangro resumed work, completely renovating the chapel, although the general architectural configuration was left intact, with a rectangular hall with small chapels along the sides. Four sixteenth-century sculptures were also left, portraits of Gianfrancesco Paolo and Paolo de' Sangro, respectively the fourth and first princes of Sansevero. The former statue is attributed to Giulio Mencaglia, the latter to Giacomo Lazzari. They are located along the left wall from the entrance. The other two statues are a bust of Alessandro de' Sangro, on the wall to the left of the altar, and a monument to Paolo de' Sangro, second prince of Sansevero, wearing the garb of a Roman centurion, to commemorate his military valor.

In 1750 Raimondo, along with Antonio Corradini, a sculptor from the Veneto, introduced a decorative program imbued with a new taste in art, which permeated the entire monument (Corradini had long been in service to Charles VI of Austria). Corradini already had a relationship with the prince, who in 1742 had commissioned him to create a bust in honor of his grandfather Paolo, sixth prince of Sansevero. This was placed in a small oval niche on the wall to the right of the entrance. The portrait is not idealized; rather, it reproduces the individual's physiognomy and characteristic features, an indication of the social power the family had achieved.

Corradini is credited with the monument to Giovan Francesco Paolo, third prince of Sansevero, on the entrance wall, to the left. Other works attributed to him are *Decorum*, in the left corner, next to the bust of Paolo, and *Modesty*, next to the right pier of the triumphal arch. The sculptor executed thirty-six busts of fired clay, which took up an entire level of the chapel. The other artists involved—from the Genoese Francesco Queirolo to Francesco Celebrano, to Paolo Persico and Francesco Maria Russo—had to conform somehow to the general design by Corradini, who was, in addition, very close to Raimondo de' Sangro because of their shared Masonic sympathies.

The space is rectangular, with four shallow chapels to the right and left. The third portal on the left is a secondary entrance, which until the nineteenth century was the only entrance to the chapel. An exit along the opposite wall descends to the circular basement-level sepulchral vault. The molding that runs along the arches of the chapel and the Corinthian capitals above were probably made from a putty-like substance invented by Raimondo. The vault was frescoed in 1749 by Francesco Maria Russo. More light used to enter from the side windows, but this was blocked by buildings erected later. The light of the Holy Spirit radiates from above and penetrates the cavity of the vault, gradually revealing the imaginary architecture depicted there. The influence of the school of Solimena can be intuited in the overall scheme.

In 1766 Francesco Celebrano created a monument to Cecco de' Sangro, which stands at the main entrance. Cecco is depicted as a tribune of the Italian regiment in Belgium and Gaul, in the act of leaping out from a coffin, wherein he had feigned death for two days, with the intention of surprising and routing the enemy. To the left of the entrance is a monument to Giovan Francesco Paolo de' Sangro, third prince of Sansevero, who died during a military expedition in Africa in 1627. This work, executed by Celebrano in 1752, groups a shell-shaped basin for holy water, a funerary stele, and an angel that covers the frame of the inscription with a veil as a sign of mourning. Next to this piece, in the corner to the left, Corradini's *Decorum* refers to the virtues

VNICVM
MILITIÆ
FVLMEN

of Isabella Tolfa and Laudonia Milano, wives of Giovan Francesco de' Sangro, who is symbolized by a young man clad in a lion's skin and wearing a single stocking, echoing a custom in the Greek world that is charged with mythological significance. Along the left side, next to the monument to Paolo de' Sangro di Mencaglia (1642), is *Liberality*, by Francesco Queirolo, dedicated to Giulia Gaetani of Aragon, wife of Paolo, fourth prince of Sansevero. The figure, wearing classical garments, holds coins and a compass in her right hand and a cornucopia with money and jewels in her left—symbols of generosity and equilibrium.

Beyond the monument to Giovan Francesco Paolo de' Sangro, first prince of Sansevero, is *Religious Zeal* (1756), by Fortunato Onelli, perhaps completed by unknown stoneworkers under the guidance of Celebrano. This work was created in memory of Ippolita del Carretto and Adriana Carafa della Spina, wives of Giovan Francesco de' Sangro. The two women's profiles are depicted in a medallion held up by two putti. The lantern and whip held by the old man symbolize, respectively, truth and heresy. The serpent emerging from the book (an erotic text), below, is the symbol of evil. The oval at the secondary entrance, beneath the arch, depicts Vincenzo de' Sangro, eighth prince of Sansevero and son of Raimondo, and was executed by Carlo Amalfi, a skilled portraitist from Sorrento, who is also the author of the painting on the tomb of Raimondo de' Sangro. Beyond the portal of the old entrance, *The Gentleness of Marital Amusement* was the last group sculpted by Paolo Persico, in 1768. It is dedicated to Gaetana Mirelli di Teora, wife of Vincenzo de' Sangro. The female figure raises two hearts in her right hand, symbols of love, while in her left she clasps the plumed "amusement," which indicates obedience. A pelican held up by a putto symbolizes charity. In the last chapel to the left is a work of simple and refined composure, Queirolo's monument to the family saint who died in 1159, Rosalia de' Sangro, who became the patron saint of Palermo. In the corner of the right pier of the triumphal arch, Corradini's *Modesty* (1752), dedicated to Raimondo's mother, Cecilia Gaetani dell'Aquila of Aragon, is a splendid figure of a woman wrapped in a transparent veil. The workmanship is extremely refined, with the cloth becoming an impalpable barrier to any corporeal contact.

The altar, executed by Francesco Celebrano after 1762, is a sort of marble relief painting, a genre that was widespread in the seventeenth and eighteenth centuries. The canopy, inserted into a shroud upheld by two angels, streams downward onto the altar, within the geometric space of the arched niche that lies behind. Beneath the arch, a putto lifts up the cover of a tomb. Above is a *Pietà* by an unknown Neapolitan artist from the sixteenth century, the oldest sacred image in the chapel.

To the sides of the altar, angels by Paolo Persico participate organically in the scene. On the right pier of the triangular arch, *Disillusionment*, by Queirolo, is dedicated to the prince's father, Antonio de' Sangro. He is portrayed in the act of freeing himself from a net, which symbolizes sin, assisted by a winged angel with a flame on its forehead, symbol of human intellect and religious ardor. Below, a terrestrial globe symbolizes human passions, and the book is the holy Bible, a Masonic symbol. The sculpted net is an extraordinary work of art by Queirolo, who had to finish it himself, using a pumice stone, since the other artisans refused to do so, out of fear of breaking it. Along the right side of the altar is *Sant'Odorisio*, in honor of the family saint who was abbot of Montecassino, and *Sincerity*, in memory of Raimondo's wife, Carlotta Gaetani dell'Aquila of Aragon. Both works by Queirolo show a refined elegance of workmanship. In her left hand, the female figure holds a heart, representing dawn and charity; in her right hand she holds a staff, a traditional attribute of Mercury and a symbol of peace and religion. The two doves below indicate purity and marital fidelity. The putto is by Paolo Persico. On the other side of the entrance is *Self-Possession*, executed by Celebrano in 1767, from a design by Queirolo. It is dedicated to Girolama Loffredo, wife of Paolo de' Sangro and paternal grandmother of Raimondo, and she is portrayed in a medallion held by a putto. A soldier holding a lion by a chain symbolizes control over brute force and impulses.

The second chapel to the right of the entrance contains a bust executed by Corradini in 1742 for Paolo de' Sangro. In front of the pier, Francesco Queirolo's *Education*, 1753, is dedicated to the memory of Girolama Caracciolo and Clarice Carafa di Stigliano, Paolo de' Sangro's first and second wives. The sculpture depicts a woman instructing a young man with Cicero's *De Officiis*.

preceding pages, left
Antonio Corradini, *Modesty*, detail.

preceding pages, right
Francesco Maria Russo, *The Glory of Paradise*, ceiling fresco.

Overall interior view of Sansevero chapel.

CISCO EX CAROLO IOHANNIS
VB PHILIPPO II·HISPANIARVM
IN BELGIO ET GALLIA SAGA
ARCE VERO AMBIANA NVCVM
FVGATISQVE INOPINATO GAL
PER CVNICVLOS DEIN IRRVENT
ET AD SPECTACVLVM ALIQVOR
IPSO MONENTE VVLGATVM
EX IGNITABVLORVM ARCA VBI IN
A SVIS ABSCONDITVS BIDVO IACVERAT
FORIBVS CLAVSIS PONTIBVS ELEVATI
ET PACEM ROGANTIBVS PACISQV
PERPETVA HOSTIVM IGNOMINIA
AD VSELLIS INSVLAM VALLVM PE
LONGE
FATO IVVENTAM ET IMMORTA
RAYMVNDVS DE SANGRO S·SEVE

NATO
NC·S·SEVERI PNPIS RIBVNO
ITALICAE LEGIO GNI
TE·ET VICTORIIS CLAM INVECTIS
RO IMPEDIMENTIS INSIGNIORI
SVBIVGATA PLANE INSIGNIORI ARCEQVE POTITIS
DENVO GALLIS ARCEQVE SVSPENDENDIS
SVIS PATIBVLO SVSPENDENTIBVS
MATIM CONFLVENTIBVS FEMORE
FLICTV VVLNERATO FEMORE
MPLO PROSILIENTI EXCVBIIS PEREMPTIS
STIBVS IMMENSO IGNE EXTERRITIS
NDITIONIBVS AB IPSO STATVTIS
NQVE MILITIBVS INDE EGREDIENTI
NISSIMO
VTANTI SCLOPI ICTV PERCVLSO
TI NOMEN CONCEDENTI
NCEPS AETERNVM POSVIT 1766

EDUCATIO
ET DISCIPLINA
MORES FACIUNT

Beyond the seventeenth-century monument to Paolo de' Sangro, in the corner to the right of the entrance is an eighteenth-century statue by an unknown artist, *Divine Love*, represented as a young man with a heart in his right hand. It is dedicated to the mystical virtues of Giovanna, wife of Giovan Francesco de' Sangro. Finally, to the right of the entrance, is a monument to Giovan Francesco, fifth prince of Sansevero, which has an angel with an epigraph, executed by Francesco Celebrano in 1756.

At the center of the nave is the *Veiled Christ*, by Giuseppe Sanmartino, a young Neapolitan sculptor. The sculptural program for the chapel called for this work, for which Antonio Corradini had made a sketch. Sanmartino created a masterpiece, quite different from Corradini's own style. The veil is an expressive vehicle through which the sculptor delineates with extraordinary precision a sort of spirit of suffering, suspended between reality and a mysterious feeling of sacredness. The veil simultaneously covers and reveals, creating a subtle,

preceding page
Francesco Celebrano, *Funerary Monument of Cecco de' Sangro*, 1766.

opposite
Francesco Queirolo, *Education*, 1753.

right
Giacomo Lazzari (attributed), *Monument to Giovan Francesco Paolo de' Sangro.*

ambiguous diaphragm that contributes to the work's continued fascination.

Opposite the old entrance, on the right side of the nave, a narrow passage, which has the chapel's original marble paving, leads to the basement-level sepulchral vault. This "espèce de caveau," as Raimondo de' Sangro himself called it, was to be expanded to accommodate the family tombs, but the project was not carried out. The prince planned to place the *Veiled Christ* at the center of the space, perpe-tually illuminated by a lamp of his own invention.

The vault contains two skeletons, a man and a woman, with the vein and artery systems largely intact, thanks to a process that remains a mystery. According to legend, these were two servants of the prince, into whose blood a liquid was injected that petrified their veins and arteries.

Overall, the sculpture and, in general, the entire marble and pictorial dec-orative apparatus of the de' Sangro chapel, responds to a precise need to hand down and celebrate the universal values of the de' Sangro family, using allusive and esoteric language. This is an apparent contrast to the Enlightenment celebration of reason, specific to the period, according to Rosanna Cioffi, and consistent with "the persistence of the sixteenth- and seventeenth-century Masonic tradition."

The true author of this extraordinary monumental space is Raimondo de' Sangro. The stylistic characteristics of the individual works, in close relationship with the artists chosen by the careful and demanding prince, help to create the legendary aura that permeates the chapel. This effect is furthered by the esoteric character attributed to every sculpture and to every element of the whole.

Hermeticism, or the desire to negate immediate comprehension of a message, which is expressed, instead, through symbols, was a Masonic characteristic and one practiced by Prince Raimondo. The first Masonic lodges in Naples were established during the period of the Austrian viceroys, with the ideas probably imported from military circles. In 1751 Pope Benedict XIV and Charles III Bourbon sought to crush the movement, and de' Sangro himself, who had become the grand master of the Neapolitan lodge, was excommunicated.

The other component of mystery that surrounds the history of the chapel and the prince has to do with Raimondo de' Sangro's strange inventions. "This gentleman is short in stature with a large head, handsome and jovial in appearance, a philosopher of the spirit, very absorbed in mechanics, extremely charming and sweet in manner, scholarly and withdrawn. He is a lover of conversation of men of learning." This was how the Enlightenment thinker Antonio Genovesi described him, although he then attributed to him the "defect of having too much imagination."

His inventions were innumerable. In 1729, only eighteen years old, he invented a retractable stage, on the occasion of festivities for the birth of the daughter of Charles VI of Austria. He also invented a waterproof fabric, a new process for plating pans in copper, and a carriage that moved in water, drawn by horses without sailors. He studied pyrotechnics so he could color flames in the most unexpected ways; he invented a machine to "lift water" and an "eternal lamp." Then there was the aforementioned feat of the two skeletons in the chapel. All these bear witness to an incredible moment in eighteenth-century aristocratic culture, when research and experimentation, carried out with popular ingenuity, approached legendary heights.

preceding page
Giuseppe Sanmartino, *Veiled Christ*, detail.

Francesco Queirolo, *Disillusionment*.

following page
Labyrinth-patterned floor, detail.

ANTONIO SANCRIO
DUCI TURRIS MAIORIS
PAULI SANSEVERI
PRINCIPIS FILIO
ELOQUENTIA INGENIO
VARIAQ·FORTUNA ADMIRABILI
QUI QUUM UXORE
IN ADOLESCENTIA AMISSA
CÆLEBS DEIN
JUVENILIBUS CUPIDITATIBUS
SATIS SUPERQ·PARUISSET
PROPTEREAQUE
PATRIA PROCUL EUROPAM OMNEM
PERAGRASSET
IDEMQ·COGNITIS
TANDEM ERRORIBUS
REDUX SACERDOS
HUIUSQ·TEMPLI ABBAS
SANCTITATE MORUM INSIGNIS
VI·ID·SEPT AN·MDCCLVII
ÆT·SUÆ LXXII OBIISSET DOCUIT
NON DATUM ESSE
HUMANÆ IMBECILLITATI
UT MAGNÆ SINE VITIIS VIRTUTES
EXISTANT
RAYMUNDUS SANSEVERI
PRINCEPS FILIUS
NE QUID PATRI NE QUID VERITATI
DENEGARET
EIUSMODI ELOGIUM
INSCRIBENDUM PONENDUMQUE
CVRAUIT
NCULA TUA
DISRUMPAM
VINCULA
TENEBRARUM
ET LONGÆ NOCT
QUIBUS ES
COMPEDITUS
UT NON CUM
HOC MUNDO
DAMNERIS
NAHUM CAP.I.
VERS. XIII.
SAPIENTIÆ
CAP. XXII.
VERS.II.
PAUL I. AD CORIN.
CAP. XI.
VERS. XXXII.
FRANCISCVS QVEIROLI

Palazzo Corigliano

Facade overlooking Piazza San Domenico Maggiore.

Bartolomeo Ranucci and Filippo Buonocore, the duke's study, detail.

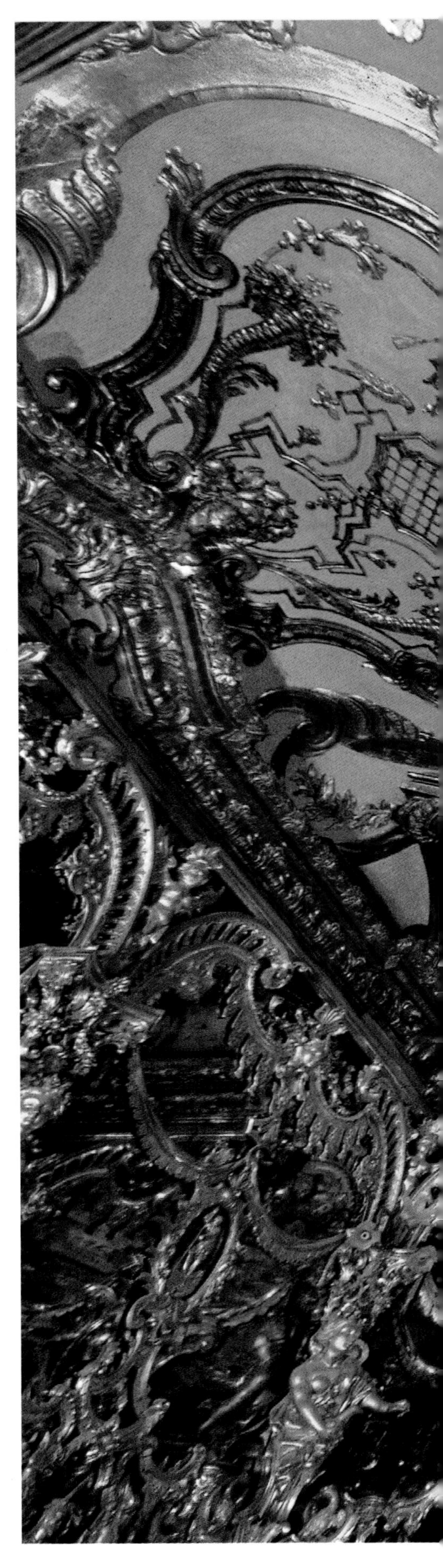

The palazzo of the dukes of Corigliano, on the south side of Piazza San Domenico Maggiore, was built in the sixteenth century for the de' Sangro family. It was probably designed by Giovanni Donadio, known as Mormando. The building later passed into the hands of the Limatola family, who definitely were living there in the late seventeenth century and continued to do so until 1725, when the family line died out. Put up for auction, the property was acquired in 1732 by Agostino Salluzzo, duke of Corigliano.

According to Bernardo Tanucci, Salluzzo belonged to "a class neither loved nor admired in Naples, the newly rich [although his] competence at business was never in question." Born in 1680, he came from a family of Genoese businessmen who, in the person of his forebear Giacomo, obtained Neapolitan citizenship in 1644. This was a typical case of purchased nobility, according to a process that allowed those from outside the realm, particularly those from Genoa, to enter the traditional ranks of the aristocracy after having

left and above
Bartolomeo Ranucci and Filippo Buonocore, the duke's study, detail.

brilliant careers in public administration.

Salluzzo was close to the Hapsburgs, as seen by his participation, with Eugene of Savoy, in the defense of Turin when it was under siege by the French in 1706, and in a battle on the Schelde River, six years later. This stood him in good favor during the brief Austrian vice-regency, which certainly did not hinder his assuming an important position under the Bourbons as well. In fact, because of his unquestionable entrepreneurial talents, in 1739 Charles made him a member of the Council of the Supreme Trade Magistracy and then a Gentleman of the Chamber, a post that allowed him access to the royal apartments.

The height of the sixteenth-century palazzo was increased one story by Filippo Buonocore, known especially as a set designer. Apart from this modification, which eliminated the attics, the facade remained substantially unaltered, except for slight changes on the second floor. The most significant intervention to the preexisting structure was on the interior, where the artist gave free reign to his imagination. The ceilings of the public rooms were covered by lathe-work, then plastered and decorated. The reception-hall ceiling had a stucco depiction of *The Fall of the Giants*; the other rooms had representations of the myths of *Atalanta and Hippomenes*, *Narcissus*, and other themes, which have now disappeared.

One of the most extraordinary spaces from eighteenth-century Europe is to be found on the third floor—the duke's study, a sort of private meditation chamber, a cube approximately five meters on each side. Its workmanship is of the highest quality, with mirrored walls with frames and gilded inlay figures by the sculptor and set designer Bartolomeo Ranucci, under the supervision of Filippo Buonocore. The space was created between 1734 and

Bartolomeo Ranucci and Filippo Buonocore, the duke's study, detail.

1741. Gian Giotto Borrelli described how "the uninterrupted use of reflected images and the enveloping line of the lacework inlay defy imagination. Even the sole balcony, necessary to ventilate the candle smoke, is an integral part of the room. Indeed, the backs of the shutters, when closed, contain a double portrait of the duke, dressed in the uniform of his highest military and civilian ranks." The four walls are divided into twelve principal sections, around which, in middle and low relief, figures compose four groups of allegories, inspired by several basic themes: the achievements of the duke, the labors of Hercules, and the gods. Fifty brackets, arranged at various heights in the inlay scheme, supported small vases of Chinese porcelain, now dispersed. The ceiling, which is inhabited by depictions of cornucopias, sphinxes, and birds, contains a central bay with Aurora, Aeolus, and Zephyr, all in gold against a light green ground. Herms in full relief, beneath the capitals, depict *The Seasons*. In the corners are depictions of *Purity, Nobility, Modesty,* and *Liberality*, along with the other Virtues, all presumably taken from Cesare Ripa's *Iconologia* (1603), which was known through numerous reprintings. A second horizontal row has some depictions that belong to the series of *Myths*, such as *Hercules Killing the Hydra*, *Apollo and Daphne*, *The Abduction of Demeter by Poseidon* and *The Abduction of Proserpine by Pluto*. This group of mythological events can be interpreted in various ways, with a common denominator of *Force and Love*. At the same height there are reliefs illustrating *Military Glories*. The last group, which can be seen as a reference to the achievements of the duke, consists of a series of ovals placed on the sidemost band. These contain representations of the reactivation of the silver mine near Corigliano, agricultural activities, and the Istituzione del Monte for young girls.

The basement-level room contains evidence of discoveries made through the excavations conducted during restoration work. It is clear that the area, while frequented since the fifth century B.C., was urbanized only in the second century B.C., after the wall of the Greek city had lost its defensive function and military character. The consequent urbanization involved the creation of a new road network aligned in a north-south direction and subsequent structural and drainage work.

Bartolomeo Ranucci and Filippo Buonocore, the duke's study, detail.

Palazzo Maddaloni

Entrance to the Palazzo *Maddaloni*, engraving, 1685 (by P. Sarnelli, *Guida dei forestieri*) or 1706 (from *Les délices d'Italie* by Rogissart, Leiden).

P. Petrini, *Palazzo Maddaloni*, engraving on copper.

The Palazzo Maddaloni, close to the Largo dello Spirito Santo, survives as evidence of an extraordinary period of building activity. Beginning in the sixteenth century, there was a construction boom along the Via Toledo, which was the new axis of development in the plan for the city's rebuilding and expansion. This plan had been implemented in the previous century by the viceroy of Philip II of Aragon, Don Pedro Alvarez di Toledo, marchese of Villafranca. Between 1530 and 1540 projects were undertaken on a vast scale. The enclosing wall was expanded, the streets freed of permanent and itinerant shopkeepers' wares. The sewage system was rebuilt and expanded. Many areas of the city, beginning with the new Via Toledo, were finally repaved. Toward the end of the century the policies imposed by the Spaniards began to have an effect. Sumptuous residences were built, alternating with modest structures, in the area close to the old royal palace, and in particular along the new street that gradually began to become the true axis of

l Palazzo del Duca di Madaloni Carafa
uga delle Stanze ui e di marauiglioso un Gabinetto teſsuto di Cristalli e dipint
o del Pó oltre l'essere mirabilmente detto palagio architettato

urban development. New structures were built for the most part by the nouveau riche class and by businessmen, who came from the surrounding territories to participate in an untitled aristocracy.

Cesare D'Avalos, marchese of Aragon, was at the center of one of these new circles, and for his own palazzo he chose a site delimited by the Via del Carogioiello (the present-day Via Tommaso Senise), the Via Toledo, and the Via Sant'Anna dei Lombardi.

On 30 October 1580 a deed under seal of notary Aniello De Martino granted Cesare D'Avalos the estate of Duke Camillo Pignatelli di Monteleone, a piece of land called "Biancomangiare" or "white food," from the presence of pastry workshops. He immediately began construction on the new building, characterized by a "C"-shaped plan, with the central facade overlooking the Via Maddaloni and the sides overlooking the Via Toledo and the Via Sant'Anna dei Lombardi.

The sloping tufacious plane located beneath the ground, between seventeen and twenty meters deep, was terraced in order to build the foundations directly on rock. By 8 January 1582 construction had advanced to the point where a contract of purchase for a piece of land mentions that it is between the church of Monteoliveto and the new Palazzo D'Avalos.

In April of that same year the marchese obtained a lease in perpetuity from the monks of Monteoliveto, for part of the "Carogioiello" terrain, which thus extended his property as far as the street of that name. In 1585 other tax assessments of land came from the Arch-confraternity of Pilgrims. Thus the building could be expanded with the closing of the fourth side along the present-day Via Senise. The later addition of this building element is evident in the lack of symmetry in the masonry compared to the preexisting sides, and in the superimpositions of vaulted structures to the elements that attach the building fabric to the ground floor. The period of greatest splendor for the palazzo began in the second half of the seventeenth century, after a quick succession of new owners: following Cesare D'Avalos were Francesco D'Avalos, the marchese of San Giuliano, Marchese Torella, Gaspare Roomer, and finally, Diomede Carafa di Maddaloni, who purchased the palazzo in 1656. He was considered "violent, haughty, and oppressive . . . and soon became disliked and hated." The new owner was described as a landed proprietor of high rank who was guilty of brutal crimes against the people and who did not hesitate to organize bands of criminals to press his demands. Masaniello accused him of treachery and

Ceiling fresco by Fedele Fischetti in the entrance vestibule.

following pages
Fencing room on the *piano nobile*.

Detail of the ballroom or dancing gallery on the *piano nobile*, which predates Fanzago's intervention, with frescoes begun by Giacomo Del Po and completed by Fedele Fischetti, around 1770. In the upper portion is a small balcony with a faux wooden railing.

requested his head, but the duke escaped to Rome, while Giuseppe Carafa and the prior of Roccella were killed.

New construction activity and the decorative wealth of some aspects of the palazzo after it passed into the hands of Diomede Carafa were an affirmation of a rediscovered dimension and renewed power on the part of this representative of the urban aristocracy. The most significant elements of the new work are attributed to Cosimo Fanzago, a native of Bergamo who did a great deal of work in Naples, leaving his unmistakable mark on the city's architecture and sculpture. During his time in Naples, Fanzago was also forced to withdraw temporarily to Rome. He committed an error in transcription when he sculpted in marble, in the Piazza Mercato, the statutes for the abolition of taxes granted by the viceroy to Masaniello, a mistake for which the people held him responsible. In any case he returned to Naples in 1651, in time to play a leading role in the most important aspects of the palazzo's construction, perhaps even before it was acquired by Diomede Carafa.

The most significant structural and architectural transformations took place prior to 1710. The entrance portal on Via Maddaloni was created; the courtyard portico opposite the entrance was built; the main staircase was expanded, assuming its present configuration; the Sala Maddaloni on the third floor, with its exterior loggia, was enlarged. The third floor was also extended, and new spaces on the fourth floor were created with structural work of significant impact, including the building of supporting masonry walls inside the existing edifice, beginning from the foundations and going down more than seventeen meters deep, and intersecting two levels of vaults.

Many external windows were transformed into balconies, following a local tradition, and "exposed" structural elements—stone columns or surfaces—were covered in plaster, stucco, and cornices. Finally the wells and cisterns were linked to the Bolla aqueduct, a branch of which passed at the level of the nearby Via Domenico Capitelli.

Cosimo Fanzago is traditionally credited with the design of the ornate portal, which can be considered a prototype for triumphal entrances in the eighteenth-century Neapolitan tradition. It is a veritable celebratory mechanism of the owners' power. The gigantic order of the rusticated pilasters continues beyond the entrance arch, to the curved broken tympanum that frames, at the center, a large oculus surmounted by a shell. The entire portal is linked to the facade through a series of architectural and decorative elements, such as the upper balcony (eighteenth century), and the reiteration of the pilasters and friezes to the sides of the entrance, which heighten the feeling in inexhaustible fantasy.

Traditionally attributed to Fanzago, the stucco friezes of the staircase, now almost completely gone, can be assigned to him with certainty.

The so-called "Sala Maddaloni," a ballroom, predated Fanzago's addition of the loggia, as can be seen in the open arched window above the opening of the loggia and in the facade on Via Tommaso Senise. The ballroom had "large square paving and ceilings of canvas with excellent paintings depicting a military action, and another illuminated by six balcony openings," according to a document dated 1811 belonging to Don Tommaso Caracciolo, prince of Colubrano.

In the late seventeenth century, Giacomo del Po replaced the painter Francesco de Maria, who was to have created the decoration of many of the palazzo's spaces. Po is responsible for the very famous "spherical hall," now

destroyed, which was located at the intersection between the edifice on Via Toledo and that on Via Senise. The artist worked in the palazzo until 1710.

From 1656 to 1806 the palazzo was subdivided between the Carafa di Maddaloni heirs, but it still remained in the family. On 21 November 1806 the last direct descendant of the duke of Maddaloni, Diomede Marzio Pacecco Carafa, sold the most significant portion of the palazzo, including the famous hall that had been at the center of so many cultural and social events, to his uncle, Don Tommaso Caracciolo, prince of Colubrano. It then passed into the hands of the prince of Avellino.

Around 1850 the palazzo was divided among the duke of Miranda, the prince of Arieniello, the prince of Ottaiano, Duke Catemario, and Count Garzilli.

Additional transformations were made, including the "Garzilli staircase" (to the left of the entrance hall between the ground floor and second floor), a passage affording access to the fourth floor on the side of the courtyard parallel to Via Maddaloni, and innumerable dormers. All contributed toward complicating the structure of this ancient noble residence.

Study, early 19th century.

Interior.

Palazzo Reale

Naples was ruled by Spanish viceroys for approximately two centuries, from the beginning of the sixteenth century until early in the eighteenth century. This was a period characterized by strong social inequality, due to Spanish policies, but also due to cultural and economic turmoil and important urban initiatives that definitively marked the development of the city and its appearance for subsequent centuries.

The Palazzo Reale stands in Piazza Plebiscito, at the end of the street opened up by Don Pedro de Toledo, viceroy in Naples from 1532 to 1553. The building, emblematic of this period on account of its intact appearance and urban position, occupies a strategic site to the west of the older city center. Domenico Fontana, the first architect of the new palazzo, reorganized the port and arsenal beyond the Castelnuovo zone, which during the vice-regency was enclosed by additional heavy fortifications.

Fontana had been in Rome in the service of Pope Sixtus V, and he had worked on the expansion of that city with an extensive project of roads that became the supporting structure for future expansions until the nineteenth century. When the pope died, Fontana fell out of favor with his successor and was called to Naples by viceroy Juan de Zuñica, count of Miranda. In 1598 Philip III inherited the Spanish throne, succeeding his father, Philip II. In 1559 the new king sent Fernandez Ruiz de Castro, count of Lemos, to be viceroy in Naples, and he entrusted Fontana with the design and building of the new palace. The city already had a palace for the viceroy, and although it was known as the "old" palace, it had been built only fifty years before, at the behest of Viceroy Don Pedro de Toledo, who had assigned that project to architects Ferdinando Manlio and Giovanni Benincasa.

Old images of the original palace, which occupied an area that separates the current Palazzo Reale from San Carlo, show a structure that is part residence, part fortress, held between two end towers (one of which was demolished by Fontana). Three rows of windows and a facade overlook the present Piazza San Ferdinando. That

Facade facing the Piazza del Plebiscito.

following page
Grand staircase.

facade curved toward the west to form a corner, toward what would be called the "Largo di Palazzo" after Fontana's building was erected. In 1540 Don Pedro de Toledo had splendid gardens placed between the old palace and the sea, probably with avenues paved in brick, some of which have been found during recent restoration. The site had been occupied previously by gardens created under Angevin rule and later destroyed during the conflict with the Durazzeschi family.

The decision to build the new palace in the same area as the old one confirms the importance of the district, which is close to the port and the sea and was thus opportune if there were a need to flee. This choice also denotes a close functional tie between the two buildings, with the new royal palace continuously expanded over the centuries, and the "old" one only demolished in 1843 during work by architect Gaetano Genovese. Work on the new palace began in 1600 and proceeded steadily throughout the rule of Viceroy Francisco de Castro (1601-03), successor to the count of Lemos. Work slowed down under Viceroy Juan Alfonso Pimentel d'Errera (1603-10), perhaps because of economic difficulties connected to Spain's wartime activities. Work resumed in 1610 with the new viceroy, Pedro Fernandez de Castro, also count of Lemos.

In 1616 the facade and courtyard were already completed, according to a description by Confalonieri, who passed through Naples: "We others went to see the structure of the royal palace, which has a facade made entirely of carved stone. On the second floor we counted twenty-one windows and three balustrades. On the ground floor there are large porticos, which look out over the street and are used by two companies of soldiers who stand sentry. . . . Inside the palazzo was not finished. It has two large staircases, a large square courtyard with porticos, two parts of which remain open, awaiting the rest of the building."

In 1604, three years after the death of Domenico Fontana, the description of the palazzo was published with the title *Dichiarazione del Nuovo Palagio cominciato nella Piazza san Luigi*. This was an appendix to a publication about the transportation of the Vatican obelisk and works executed for Sixtus V; it was reprinted that same year. For unknown reasons, the greatest engineer in the realm did not include the drawings for the project, but we can get some idea from the plan published in Rome by Giovan Giacomo De Rossi, in the first half of the seventeenth century. One can clearly detect the square Cortile d'Onore, with a double-flight staircase at the left, the spaces along the principal facade overlooking the "Largo di Palazzo," and those on the south side. The west side assumes a "C"-shape, open toward the sea, according to a formula that was somewhat common in Naples, where monastery cloisters sometimes repeat this arrangement, dictated by their specific position in the landscape.

At the end of the second decade of the eighteenth century, many of the interior spaces were finished, frescoed by Battistello Caracciolo, Giovanni Balducci, and Belisario Corenzio.

In 1644 Francesco Antonio Picchiatti had organized a competition for the decoration of the royal chapel, which was also completed. The same architect created a monumental staircase on the site of a preexisting, double-ramp staircase built under Fontana. The new staircase, called "the most beautiful in Europe" by Montesquieu in 1729, remained intact even through the nineteenth-century building project under the direction of architect Gaetano Genovese. It had a central flight that, from the first landing, broke into two opposite flights along the back wall. These flights served to separate the religious processions, which were directed along the flight of stairs to the right, toward the chapel, from secular retinues, which proceeded to the left, toward the reception hall and audience rooms. The steps then turned at a right angle on both sides to reach the level above the portico of the Cortile d'Onore. Access to the staircase was not closed off by a portico, as is clearly shown in a painting of 1790 by Antonio Dominici, who enlivened the scene with a crowd of courtesans, knights, and common people. The space, covered by a hip roof and animated by an uninterrupted series of arcades that face onto the stairs, remained closed off on the north side until the demolition of the viceroy's palace during Genovese's project.

With the advent of Bourbon rule in 1734, King Charles, unlike his predecessors, lived in the new Palazzo Reale. On the occasion of his marriage to Maria Amalia of Saxony, in 1738, he had many rooms renovated, bringing in, among others, Francesco de Mura to fresco the diplomatic hall, and Domenico Antonio Vaccaro to work on the wedding hall. However, King Charles, who was engaged in the creation of new palaces in Capodimonte, Portici, and Caserta, did not significantly increase work on the palace in Naples. But his son Ferdinand IV did resume work more intensely. In 1768, on the occasion of his marriage to Maria Carolina of Austria, the great hall created by the Spanish viceroys was transformed into a court theater by Ferdinando Fuga. During the second half of the eighteenth century the so-called "Braccio Nuovo," or new wing, was also created, on

the east side of the building. Its spaces, originally earmarked for festivities, have been occupied by the Biblioteca Nazionale Vittorio Emanuele III since 1927. This is one of the most important conservation libraries in the world, and the foremost library for the literature of southern Italy. During the first half of the eighteenth century, work was done on the facade overlooking the sea, where architect Ferdinando Sanfelice created a building element set at a slant, to be used as a carriage house. This was renovated in 1832 by Passero, who aligned it to the other wings of the palace.

The complex was definitively completed by 1843, by architect Gaetano Genovese, while the "Largo di Palazzo" was laid out in the shape of a colonnaded "forum" by architect Leopoldo Laperuta and continued by Pietro Bianchi, with the inclusion of the church of San Francesco di Paola. After the old viceroy's palace was torn down, between 1838 and 1840, Genovese created the facade and garden overlooking the Piazza Trieste e Trento. The large windows of the staircase volume on this facade opened up a perspective that, through an analogous opening on the opposite facade, crosses the Cortile d'Onore and arrives, beyond the Belvedere Courtyard, at the edge of the sea. Genovese's "C"-shaped facade was linked to the San Carlo theater by architects Francesco Gauvadan and Carlo Gesuè. Genovese was responsible for various interior consolidations (the roof) and finishings (the marble for the grand staircase), as well as the solution of the view overlooking the sea, resolved in a way that is close to the solution proposed earlier by Tuscan architect Antonio Niccolini in 1812.

One of the most significant elements of the new seventeenth-century palazzo is the facade facing the Piazza Plebiscito, articulated on three levels separated by robust cornices with broad terraces to the right and left, with a series of uninterrupted arcades on the ground level. The two upper bays, with windows with alternating curved and triangular tympanums, are framed by vertical stone pilasters, which, with the horizontal cornices, define a continuous module. The arched openings on the ground floor, the modular repetition, the absence of a strongly projecting cornice at the top and the subtlety of the entrances flanked by Doric columns (doubled only at the sides of the central entrance), with balconies above, give an overall effect of dematerialization. In the past, this was accentuated by alternating small obelisks and vases on the upper coping, which tended to negate the peremptory nature of the horizontal conclusion of the building. Today, these decorative elements, along with two clocks placed on axis with the side entrances, have disappeared, and consequently one can only partially perceive the negation of the structural logic derived from the emptying out of the ground-level arcades. In fact, because of extensive damage, which is still visible, in 1754 these were alternately filled in by Luigi Vanvitelli, who created a niche in every closed-off space, in order to maintain a chiaroscuro effect. In 1888 statues of the kings of Naples were placed in the niches, but they are out of scale with the eighteenth-century setting. From the viewer's left, these portray: *Roger the Norman* by Emilio Franceschi, *Frederick II von Hohenstaufen* by Emanuele Caggiano, *Charles I of Anjou* by Tommaso Solari, *Alfonso I of Aragon* by Achille d'Orsi, *Emperor Charles V* from a model by Vincenzo Gemito, *Charles III Bourbon* by Raffaele Belliazzi, *Joachim Murat* by Giovan Battista Amendola, and *Victor*

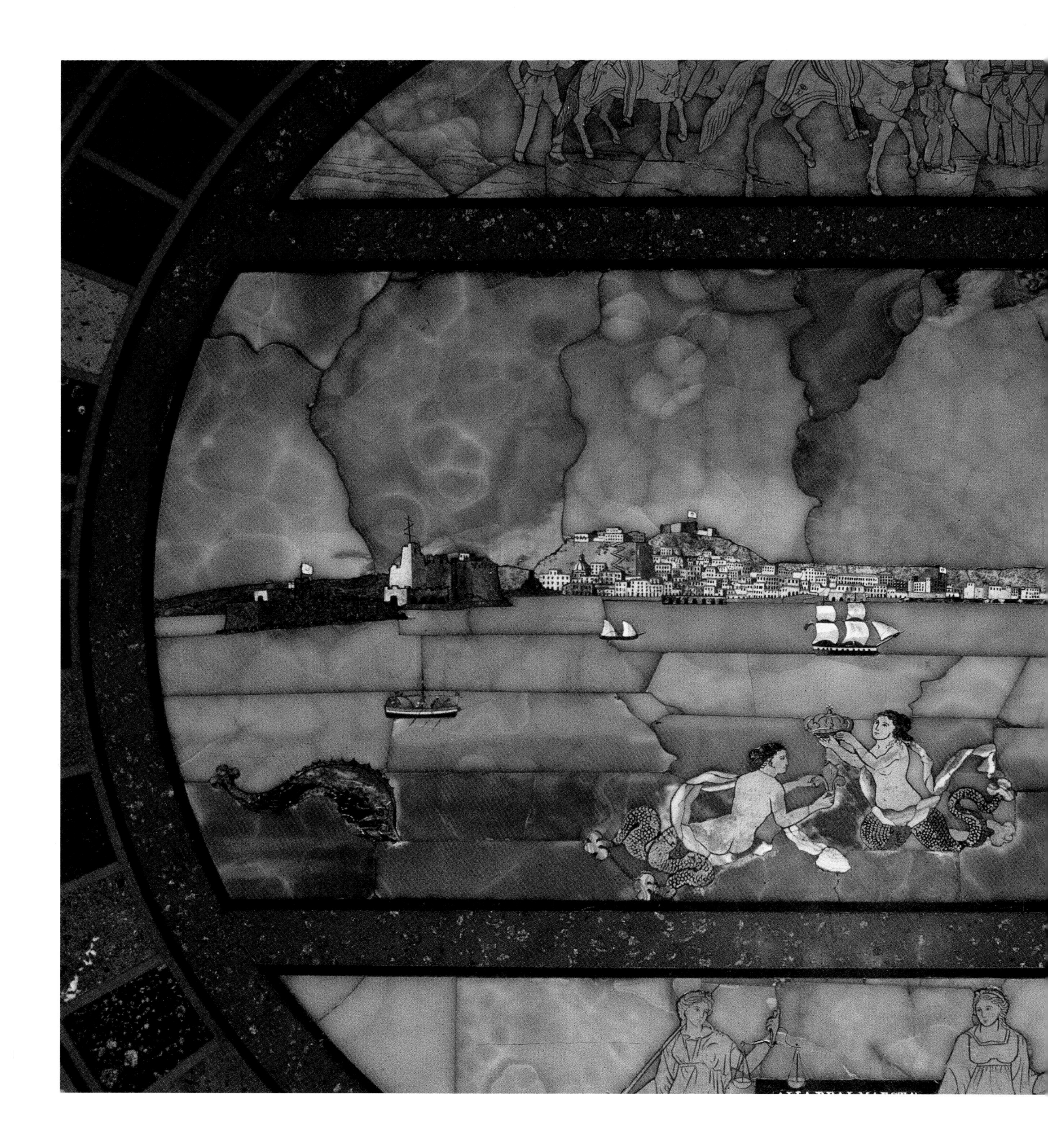

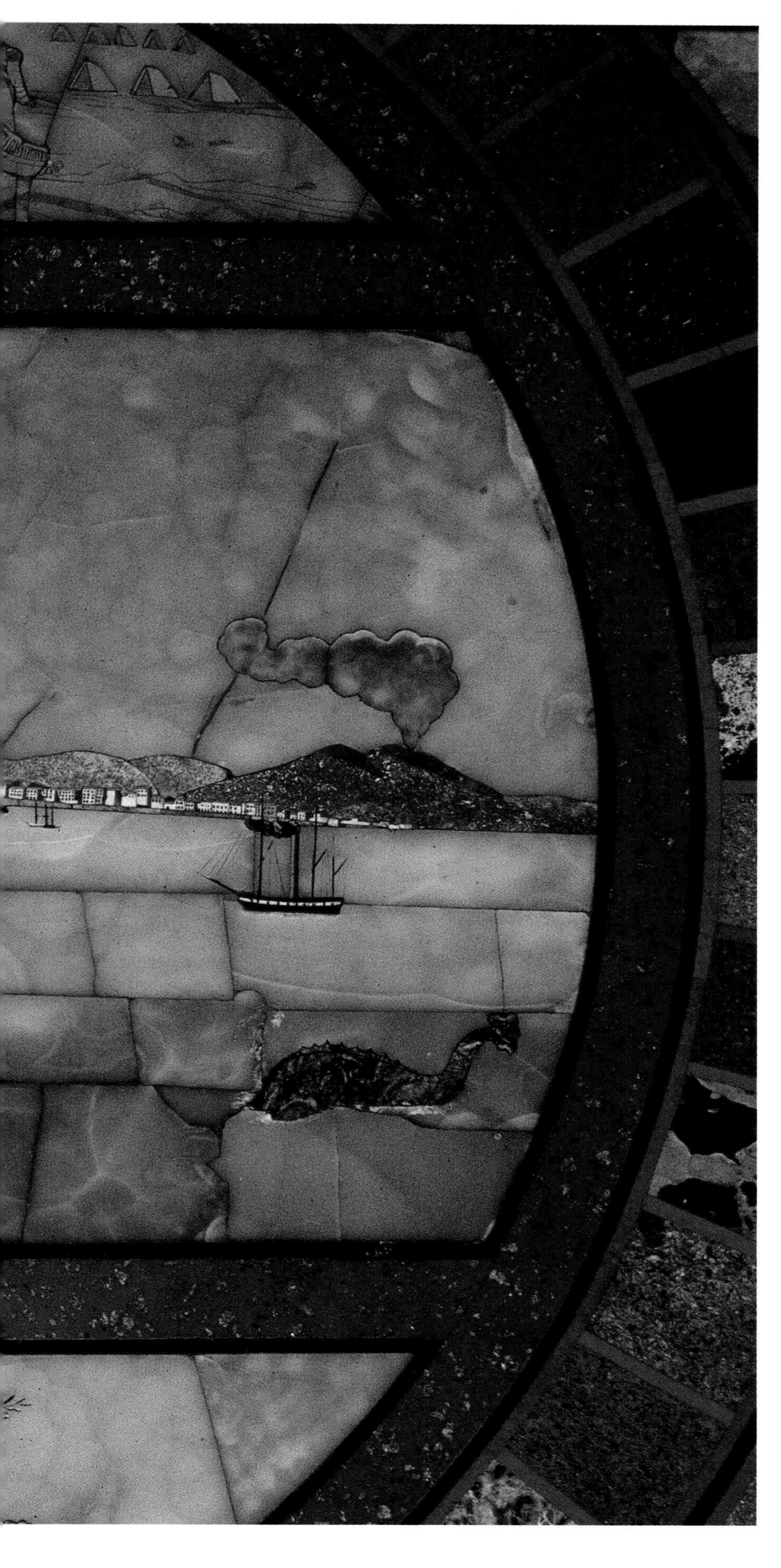

Emmanuel II of Savoy by Francesco Jerace.

The central entrance on the Piazza Plebiscito leads to the Cortile d'Onore. In 1840 Fortuna's fountain was moved to the east side of the portico, opposite the entrance, against the backdrop of a broad niche, which previously contained a simple basin.

The stone arcades separated by Doric pilasters are surmounted, in the upper order, by analogous openings alternating with Ionic pilasters, which were closed off by Genovese in the nineteenth century with neoclassical-style iron windows. Horizontal bands, with metopes and heraldic motifs from the Spanish royal house, frame both levels. The left corner of the east side of the Cortile d'Onore leads to the garden. Along the avenue that borders the garden, through an entrance porch to the right, is the Cortile delle Carrozze. This was revamped from the earlier eighteenth-century space and now contains the carriage houses, a long space with nine neo-Doric columns at the center, linked by segmented arches that define a series of bays covered by domed vaults. In 1837 Genovese modified the windows of this space so they would conform to those of the Belvedere courtyard.

In 1842 a "country" garden was created by botanist Frederick Dehnhardt, with flower beds and winding paths, and with exotic plants next to traditional species, to create specific perspectival effects and chromatic juxtapositions. The entire garden was surrounded by a railing with gilded points, curved in a semicircle with the gate in the center portion, corresponding to the entrance. In the 1920s the garden was expanded by Camillo Guerra, who in 1924 created the central slope on axis with the entrance.

Returning to the Cortile d'Onore and ascending the monumental staircase, one arrives at the luminous ambulatory, the large windows of which look out on the courtyard, repeating, in the whiteness of the neoclassical stuccowork the rhythm and course of the portico below. The court theater and the audience rooms, which face out on the Piazza Plebiscito, are located in the first wing to the right.

preceding pages, left
Hall of the Ambassadors, Antica Galleria: overall view showing the tapestries on the walls.

preceding pages, left
Hall of the Ambassadors, Antica Galleria: ceiling fresco, subdivided into fourteen compartments with gilded stucco frames alternating with coats of arms and grottesques, attributed to Belisario Corenzio and his workshop, 1620s.

G. B. Calì da Catania, detail of table top with view of Naples from the sea, made from mixed marbles, c. 1830.

In Ferdinando Fuga's court theater, which contained works by Paisiello and Cimarosa, papier-mâché statues by Angelo Viva depict *Minerva, Mercury,* and *Apollo with the Nine Muses*, placed in stucco niches interspersed with fluted pilasters. The pavilion ceiling had eighteenth-century frescoes by Antonio Dominici, including *The Marriage of Poseidon and Amphitrite*, destroyed by bombs during World War II and repainted between 1950 and 1954.

The oldest part of the building on the first floor is the royal apartment, which was occupied by the Spanish and Austrian viceroys and then by the Bourbon kings. This is still the original layout seen in the plan printed by De Rossi in the mid-seventeenth century.

The theater leads to three antechambers and then to the throne room, which is part of the royal apartment. In the first antechamber, the diplomatic hall, an earlier Mannerist ceiling painting was replaced by a fresco by Francesco de Mura. Depictions of *Royal Genius* and *Allegory of the Virtues of Charles and Maria Amalia (Fortitude, Justice, Clemency, Magnanimity, Loyalty, Prudence, and Beauty)* and *Hymen, God of Marriage, Expelling Rage, and Magnanimity* are interspersed with decorative painting by Vincenzo Re. Two early-eighteenth-century Gobelin tapestries on the walls depict *Allegories of the Elements (Air and Fire)* in celebration of the Sun king.

The ceiling of the second antechamber depicts the *Magnificence of Alfonso of Aragon* by Belisario Corenzio and his workshop, dated 1622. The long Hall of the Ambassadors also has paintings by the same artists.

The furnishings consist of Neapolitan consoles from 1780 and Chinese porcelain. The painting of *The Investiture of Saint Aspreno* is by Massimo Stanzione. The third antechamber has a ceiling fresco by Giuseppe Cammarano, depicting *Minerva Rewards Fidelity*, painted in 1818. On the central wall, the tapestry with the *Rape of Proserpine* by Pietro Duranti was executed during the period when Luigi Vanvitelli was overseeing the decorative scheme. In the throne room, an eighteenth-century baldacchino from the royal palace in Palermo overhangs the Empire-style throne (1845-50) to which the Swabian eagle was later added. The neoclassical ceiling by Antonio De Simone, dated around 1818, depicts a symbolic rendering of the extension of the reign of the two Sicilies through the female figures of the *Twelve Provinces*, and a horse and Trinacria, representing Naples and Sicily respectively. Portraits of court personalities and ambassadors hang on the walls. The adjacent "passage of the general" contains a series of canvases by Tommaso de Vivo, inspired by *Scenes from the Life of Judith* (1841-48).

Finally the gallery, known as the Hall of the Ambassadors, has several compartments, separated by stucco frames, depicting the *Splendors of the House of Spain* with *Scenes from the Life of Ferrante of Aragon*, frescoed by Belisario Corenzio and Onofrio and Andrea de Lione.

Most of the furnishings are from the early nineteenth century, in Neapolitan Empire style, with tapestries from the French school on the walls. Also noteworthy is a painting by Artemisia Gentileschi, *The Annunciation*, dated 1631.

With the coming of the Bourbons, the architecture and decoration of the interiors focused for the most part on the person of the king. In the passageways adjacent to the no longer recognizable alcove of Maria Amalia of Saxony, a work by Domenico Antonio Vaccaro painted in 1738 typifies the rococo period. *Her Royal Majesty Supported by Peace, Fortune, and Dominion* is depicted in the study to the left, while in the small room to the right is *The Holy Spirit Blessing Marriage*. In the adjacent room, also part of the queen's suite, the ceiling is decorated with white and gold stuccowork from the eighteenth century. The rooms behind open onto the wing of the ambulatory, with white lacquered doors dating to 1830, in neoclassical style. The interior doors are from

preceding pages, left
Pietro Durante (from a cartoon by Gerolamo Starace Franchis), *The Rape of Proserpine*, Royal Tapestry Factory of Naples.

preceding pages, right
Room XIV (fourth room of the *Quadreria*, or picture gallery, of Ferdinand IV, early 19th century), with two paintings by Luca Giordano, *The Five Patron Saints and San Gennaro Interceding against the Plague of 1656*. On the door to the left, an oval oil painting by Fedele Fischetti depicts *San Gennaro in a Glory of Angels*.

Second anteroom.

IV

the late eighteenth century and are richly decorated with fantastic figures of animals and shells against a gold ground.

The old private rooms have been moved to the modern corner area at the end of the reception rooms. They date back to the period of the viceroys and also include the bedchamber of Charles III Bourbon; this later belonged to Ferdinand IV and was located in the modern area of the Belvedere, which was demolished during the work carried out by Genovese. Francesco de Mura painted the ceiling of the room of Maria Cristina, but the fresco was destroyed during the military occupation. The walls of the adjacent small oratory contain five canvases by Felice Liani (1760) on the theme of the Nativity. In the *boudoir*, on the ceiling of the hip roof, are *Scenes from the Life of Consalvo da Cordova* by Battistello Caracciolo, probably commissioned by the Spanish viceroy between 1610 and 1616, and depicting the Spanish military conquest of 1502. This room also has a tapestry by Pietro Duranti, taken from a drawing by Francesco de Mura that was based on a decorative program by Ferdinando Fuga. The two

preceding page
Detail, ceiling decoration in one of the rooms of Queen Maria Amalia, by an unknown Neapolitan stucco-worker.

Palatine Chapel: apse and altar by Dionisio Lazzari, created by Neapolitan and Tuscan workmen, second half of the 17th century.

Palatine Chapel: altar inlay work, detail.

interior corner rooms between the modern wing and the long south-facing facade contain frescoes by Gennaro Maldarelli and Giuseppe Cammarano, part of Genovese's new nineteenth-century reorganization. The rooms of the so-called *Quadreria*, or picture gallery, have a series of paintings with varied provenances. These range from the seventeenth- and eighteenth-century Neapolitan school paintings (including *Orpheus and the Bacchantes* and the *Meeting of Rachel and Jacob* by Domenico Antonio Vaccaro and two large altarpieces by Luca Giordano from the church of Santa Maria del Pianto, to an *Imaginary View* by Viviano Codazzi, decorative paintings by Peter Muller, and a *View of the Spanish Royal Palaces* by Antonio Joli, in the Sala dei Paesaggi. The next room has paintings from the Baroque period by Luca Giordano, and a subsequent room has Mattia Preti's masterpiece, *The Return of the Prodigal Son*. Other rooms contain seventeenth-century paintings from Emilia. In the corner is a large ballroom, called the Hall of Hercules, once known as the Hall of the Viceroys. The patrimony of furnishings in the royal apartment, only a small portion of which has been described, is not made up of distinct collections. However, various areas can be discerned, such as Neapolitan cabinetry from the eighteenth and nineteenth centuries and a lot of furniture brought in by Joachim Murat. There are also French and Neapolitan carpets and tapestries. The porcelains include monumental Empire-style Sèvres vases and Russian and Chinese pieces that were royal gifts, as well as items made in Naples. Finally, some of the most precious furnishings include clocks, particularly Thuret's Farnese *Atlas* and Clay's musical machine from 1730. The royal chapel, where sacred furnishings are exhibited, contains a splendid Baroque altar by Dionisio Lazzari, with semiprecious stone decoration.

Detail of pictorial decoration, door between rooms XIII and XIV.

Detail of pictorial decoration, a door in the Hall of Hercules.

Palazzo Donn'Anna

"In Naples, at the end of Mergellina, about two-thirds of the way up the Posillipo hill road, which at the time of which we are speaking was a path, barely accessible by carriage, there is a strange ruin. It was built on some rocks that are continually beaten by the waves, which, during the tides, penetrate as far as its lower rooms. The ruin is strange because it is of a palazzo never brought to completion, having arrived at a state of decay without having ever passed through life. In Naples, despite denials from its seventeenth-century architect, people have named the Mergellina ruin the Palazzo of Queen Giovanna.

"But the palazzo, built two hundred years after the reign of the brazen Angevin queen, was not built by the murderous bride of Andrea and adulterous lover of Sergianni Caracciolo. Rather, it was built by Anna Carafa, wife of the duke of Medina, the favorite of Duke Olivares, known as the count-duke, who in turn was the favorite of King Philip IV. When Olivares fell from favor he brought down with him the duke of Medina

View of the palazzo from the sea.

following pages, left
Detail of the east corner, with alternating niches and balconies.

following pages, right
Loggia overlooking the sea.

Dockyard carved out of foundation structure.

The old theater overlooking the sea, now the offices of architects Sbriziolo and de Felice.

following pages
Panorama

who, recalled to Madrid, left his wife in Naples.

"The Neapolitans, who complained as long as the disgraced viceroy remained in power, pursued him in the person of his wife. Thus Anna Carafa, bruised by the contempt of the aristocracy and subjected to the insults of the populace, abandoned Naples and went to die in Portici, leaving her palazzo half-built, a symbol of the changing vicissitudes of life.

"From then on, the people spread pernicious superstitions about this stone giant. Although the Neapolitan imagination has little predilection for gloomy northern poetry and its phantasms, habitually accompanied by mist, it also avoids the limpid and transparent air of modernity. Accordingly, this ruin was said to be populated by unknown and evil spirits. They would cast the evil eye on those who were incredulous or bold enough to venture into the skeleton of a palazzo, or on those who, even more audaciously, sought to complete the structure, despite the curse that weighed upon it and despite the sea that increasingly took it over. It seemed as though the immobile and sensitive walls had inherited human passions, or that the vindictive spirits of Medina and Anna Carafa had returned, after death, to their deserted and decaying dwelling, which they had been unable to inhabit in life.

"This superstition was still being spread in mid-1798, with stories circulating particularly among the people of Mergellina, the place closest to the lugubrious site. People said that for some time, noises of chains and wails could be heard in the palazzo of Queen Giovanna; they said that, through the open windows, beneath the gloomy arcades, pale blue lights could be seen, racing through the damp, uninhabited rooms. Finally people said—according to an old fisherman, Basso Tomeo, who was blindly believed—the ruins had become a haunt for criminals."

The above excerpt from Alexandre Dumas' *La Sanfelice* effectively describes the significance that the collective imagination has always attributed to this great unfinished building:

"In 1642 Viceroy Ramino Guzman and his wife Anna

MATEMATICA

Carafa decided to tear down the sixteenth-century villa of the Bonifacio family, to construct, on the same site, a large palazzo. It was designed so that it could be reached either by sea or by carriage, from a road that was about to open, running along the coast of Posillipo." Thus begins Roberto Pane's history of the great structure. The project was entrusted to Cosimo Fanzago, who, since 1638, had been putting on theatrical spectacles in the preexisting "palazzo of the siren."

Work probably began toward the end of the 1630s, and royal architect Bartolomeo Picchiatti also ended up being involved, signing authorizations for the materials to be taken by Fanzago. In 1642, Fanzago hired Viviano Codazzi to execute an elevation of the "palazzo of his Excellence of Posillipo."

Work was interrupted by the departure of the duke of Medina Las Torre from Naples, on 25 October 1645, to be replaced by the admiral of Castiglia. The palazzo was damaged during the riots connected to the Masaniello revolution in 1647, and then by the earthquake of 1688 and its aftershocks. In 1711 partial renovation was carried out by Carlo Mirelli, marchese of Teora, as recorded in an inscription on the central arch of the facade facing the sea.

In 1812 the French expanded the Posillipo road, and parts of the facade and some spaces on the east side of the building were demolished. During the nineteenth century the building underwent numerous changes of ownership, with consequent changes of use. In 1824 a glass factory was set up. In 1870 the building was sold by the Manzi family to the Italian Construction Society, which then sold it to Marchese Geisser. The latter sought to transform it into a hotel. Acquired by the Banca d'Italia in 1896, two years later it was purchased by Genevois, who began remodeling, based on a design by engineer Guglielmo Giordano, during which the central reception hall was demolished. After considerable polemics, which involved the architect Nicola Breglia, work was resumed by architect Adolfo Avena in 1904, then again in 1911.

Although incomplete, the building still conveys the theatrical quality that Fanzago had desired. This is because his design was carefully coordinated to the site, where the sea acted as backdrop to the stage, installed between three arcades on the second floor of the main facade. Part of the vault-covered space was carved into the tufa stone; on the side opposite the arcade, the theater was screened off by a triforium wall, through which one could see the

Interior of a private residence.

water channel winding beneath the structure. The design of the serlian triforium was also carried over to the side walls, with simple stucco reliefs. The two corners of the facade overlooking the sea are rounded and lightened by terraces open to the view. The interior courtyard is accessible from the Via Posillipo.

The walls of the imposing structure are articulated in three bands, separated by alternating niches and balconies, with superimposed pilasters, outlined on the lower level. The variety of openings and the diversity of the masonry perimeter on the upper floor, in contrast to the lower ones, along with the unfinished nature of the building, imbue the project with the particular charm of an architecture suspended in a realm somewhere between impossible completion and a stage set, open to the imagination.

Private apartment.
Detail of tile floor, made in Naples, 18th century.

Palazzo Sanfelice and Palazzo dello Spagnolo

The rear staircase facade, overlooking the garden.

The first entrance.

following page
The open staircase, overlooking the interior courtyard.

The open staircases of Sanfelice give a theatrical "twist" to a tradition that has been present in Naples since the sixteenth century. But the two-dimensional stone pilasters and arches of two centuries earlier have been replaced here with a new concept of space. Space is no longer considered in terms of the rhythm of light and dark areas transposed pictorially into surfaces, as a projection of three dimensions. The Sanfelice staircases are three-dimensional structures, organic participants in an overall urban plan that, through the repetitiousness of the scheme, becomes a typological constant in the city. Along the entrance axis—entrance porch, courtyard, open stairway, garden—the space that is lacking on the outside, because of the narrow dimensions of the street, is regained on the interior of the building, as if by compensation.

The Palazzo Sanfelice was created by Ferdinando Sanfelice for his family. In the facade, ornamented with busts and rococo stuccowork, two portals lead to two parts of the building.

Matteo Egizio, a celebrated man of letters, mentioned these entrances, as well as Sanfelice's name, in his writings, one of which is dated 1728.

The back of the rectangular courtyard is taken up by an open staircase, a structure articulated over four continuous piers linked by ramps and landings, where the intrados of the arches help to heighten the continuity of the whole. It is a veritable symphony of spaces interconnected by a harmonic rhythm and overall structural geometry. The stuccowork that embellished the structures has almost completely vanished. Beyond the staircase there was a garden, so that the structure used to function as a stage set, visually integrated with the natural element, thus taking advantage of the perspectival axis that stretched from the portal to the area of vegetation.

The left portal leads to an octagonal courtyard ornamented by masks and rococo decorations. Here the staircase seems strongly geometric, carried out in a different manner from and on a larger scale than in San Giovanni a Carbonara.

Important works of art, which no longer exist, were once housed in the Palazzo Sanfelice. These included marble sculptures from the Sanmartino workshop, located in the former chapel, and the decoration of the gallery by Solimena, who was Sanfelice's teacher and friend.

Palazzo dello Spagnolo was built by Sanfelice in 1738 for Nicola Moscati. In the nineteenth century the building was purchased by a Spanish nobleman, Don Tommaso Atienza and thereafter was known by this owner's nationality.

The staircase, while different in form from that of the Palazzo Sanfelice, is also open. The vertical supports in this case are even more slender, and the voids are shaped with curved enclosing lines that accentuate the staircase's theatrical character, visually emptying the entire facade of its structural contents. The stuccowork, nearly intact, was designed by Giuseppe Astarita and fully reflects Neapolitan rococo taste, which at this point was extraneous to Sanfelice's mature style.

Palazzo dello Spagnolo: staircase looking out over the courtyard.

The open staircase, overlooking the interior courtyard.

Palazzo Serra di Cassano

The Palazzo Serra di Cassano, designed by Ferdinando Sanfelice, is located on the Via Egiziaca in Pizzofalcone. The monumental entrance consists of a broad arched doorway, articulated by Doric pilasters. The entrance leads directly into a large octagonal courtyard, which stands before a monumental staircase. The four smaller sides of the courtyard contain service stairways. The entrance door has been closed since 1799, a sign of mourning after the death of Gennaro Serra, son of the prince, killed as a participant in the Neapolitan revolution.

The present entrance to the palazzo is at the back, on the Via Monte di Dio. The facade on that street is divided by Corinthian pilasters that rest on a tall stone base. Two of the seven bays are occupied by two entrance doors, with a rusticated band in high relief and anthropomorphic capitals, above which are balconies. This entrance also leads to the large octagonal courtyard, by way of a series of entrance porches and another porticoed courtyard.

A broad arcade, now filled in with windows, links

The rear facade on Via Monte di Dio.

the courtyard with the space of the grand staircase, the building's most significant architectural element. It is a true bravura creation by Sanfelice, who succeeded in creating a harmonious whole, perfectly consistent in its language, yet within a context that is quite different from the open staircases of other palazzi, such as those of his own family or the Palazzo dello Spagnolo. Indeed, these latter have staircases that are organized as a function of the landings that lead to the various apartments, and the general layout takes advantage of the repetitiousness of the sloping flights of steps, the intervening landings, and the balustrades, which define the rhythm of the interior facade. In the Palazzo Serra di Cassano the staircase element is everything and presents a unified image in its three-dimensional and volumetric consistency. There is a particularly beautiful contrast between the stone of the staircase structures and the white reliefs and marble balustrades, which provide a continuous crown resembling lacework for the gray stone structures.

opposite
The large glassed-in arch leading to the monumental staircase of the octagonal courtyard.

left
Detail of the interior facade of the octagonal courtyard.

following page
Monumental staircase by Ferdinando Sanfelice.

The interior is characterized by opulent rooms that now house the Institute for Philosophical Studies.

The great entrance hall, which has eighteenth-century trompe-l'oeil decorations, leads to a room with monochromatic landscapes frescoed on the walls, and then to the large "hall of mirrors."

Works of art in the other rooms include paintings by Giacinto Diano, created between 1770 and 1773, in stucco frames. Nicola Spinosa has commented on the "formal qualities and compositional clarity" of one of these, *Aeneas and Ascanius in Carthage*. There is also a work by Alessandro Tiarini and, in a room devoted to Mattia Preti's work, *The Judgment of Solomon*, within a stucco "altar frame" on the wall. The secretary's office contains a painting of a religious subject attributed to Fabrizio Santafede.

Details of frescoes with *trompe-l'oeil* perspectives.

Palazzo Reale di Capodimonte
(Royal Palace at Capodimonte)

The Palazzo di Capodimonte is one of the projects undertaken by the Bourbons to further open up the city to the surrounding territory. This policy also encouraged the siting of residences away from the urban center, so king and court could enjoy their favorite pastimes, such as hunting.

The building appears as a large block with three courtyards. The red facades are divided horizontally into two areas and set back vertically by superimposed stone pilasters, terminating in spheres above the eaves of the roof line. Both as a whole and in its details, the building is extremely heavy and of modest architectural quality.

The construction history is closely linked to the arrival in Naples of Charles III Bourbon, who, as son of Elisabeth Farnese and Philip V of Spain, acceded to the throne of the kingdom of Naples in 1734.

The king had inherited form his mother the prestigious Farnese collection—paintings, drawings, books, bronzes, furnishings, cameos, coins, medallions, and numerous

The principal facade of the Palazzo Reale.

Park: the entrance to the Palazzo Reale di Capodimonte with five radiating avenues, by Ferdinando Sanfelice.

archaeological objects. Since 1725, he had planned to transfer this immense collection from his palaces in Parma and Piacenza to Naples.

Thus in 1735, both to organize part of the collection and to placate the demands of the court, Charles engaged the Palermitan architect Giovanni Antonio Medrano. He was asked to come up with a plan for purchasing lands and estates in the area and to design a new palace, to be built on the hill of Capodimonte, within a dense wooded zone, on a site overlooking the city. Medrano was briefly assisted in these tasks by a Roman architect, Antonio Canevari. Medrano presented three plans, and the one chosen is now in the Museo di Capodimonte, signed with the letter "C." It is not very dissimilar to the present building, except that a principal double-ramped staircase, planned for the central courtyard, was never built. This element, as Giancarlo Alisio has noted, would have contradicted the interpenetration of spaces on the ground floor, a feature that was one of the finest qualities of the completed building.

The work was done by the royal building contractor, Angelo Carasale, who was later arrested for illicit activity. After the confiscation of neighboring lands and the demolition of some estates, construction began in September 1738, when there was an official ceremony for the laying of the first stone. There were numerous technical problems, stemming from, among other things, difficulties in transporting materials to an area that was fairly inaccessible and rough.

Palazzo Reale di Capodimonte, now the Museo Nazionale di Capodimonte: Antonio Canova, *Letizia Ramolino Bonaparte*, plaster, early 19th century.

J. Bar, *Portrait of Fra' Luca Pacioli*, 1495.

Nonetheless, the initial work proceeded rapidly. Crates containing works from the Farnese collection—sent to Naples by sea from Genoa, beginning in 1736—were stored temporarily in the Palazzo Reale at the center of the city.

From 1742 to 1745 King Charles assigned Neapolitan architect Ferdinando Sanfelice the task of designing the layout of certain areas of the park, transforming a small building in the woods, adapting it to accommodate the Royal Porcelain Factory, and building a church to be dedicated to San Gennaro. The creation of the overall design of the park, generally attributed to Sanfelice, suffered long interruptions between 1763 and 1766, when work was resumed under the direction of architect Ferdinando Fuga. The woodland of Capodimonte, created above all to satisfy the hunting needs of the king and his court, represents a successful marriage between English romantic and Italian geometric garden design. The layout, structured by an elliptical open area, from which five long avenues depart, was originally embellished with numerous little streets and fountains. Of these, twelve sculptures survive today, depicting the months of the year, all now without heads, and a statue of a *Giant* or perhaps *Hercules*, made up of ancient fragments from the Farnese collection. But construction on the palace soon came to a halt, for technical and economic reasons, and perhaps also because of lack of interest on the part of the king, accentuated by his departure for Spain in 1759. His successor and son, Ferdinand IV (with Bernardo

following pages, left
The "porcelain room," originally in the royal palace in Portici (1757-59), contains work made at the Royal Porcelain Factory at Capodimonte.

following pages, right
Detail of the "porcelain room," with work made in the Royal Porcelain Factory at Capodimonte.

EVCLIDES.

Tanucci as his regent), preferred the new royal palace in Caserta. In the meantime, in 1758 Father Giovanni Maria della Torre organized the Farnese collection on the *piano nobile* of the Palazzo di Capodimonte, in the rooms around the south courtyard, the only completed portions at that point. Despite the building's unfinished state, many famous European cultural figures came to visit— Winckelmann, Sade, Goethe, and Canova—to admire the masterpieces on display. In 1760 work was taken up again, under the direction of Ferdinando Fuga, and a decision was made to expand the building around the central courtyard, which would not be completed, with its north side, until the fourth decade of the following century.

Political events intervened at the close of the eighteenth century with the arrival of French troops in 1799 and the consequent transfer of Ferdinand IV to Palermo. This marked the beginning of a period of great adversity, particularly for the paintings in the collection, which were confiscated and brought to Rome, but also for the palace itself and the surrounding buildings, which were sacked, and for the park, where numerous trees were destroyed.

With the return of the Bourbons from Sicily the following year, Domenico Venuti was assigned the task

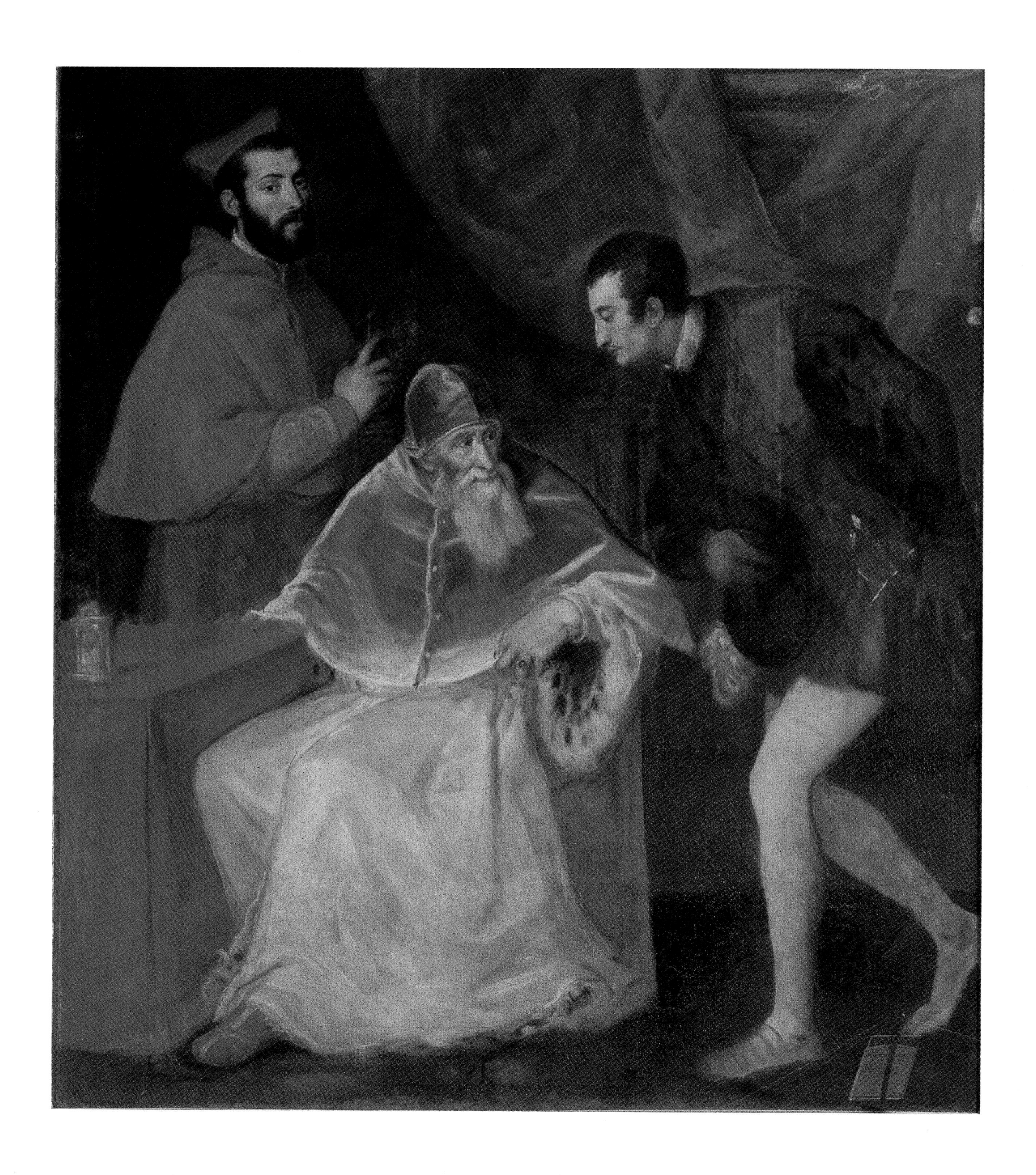

of recovering the dispersed artworks, which, along with new acquisitions and gifts, were being gathered in the palazzo of the princes of Francavilla, near the Porta di Chiaia. The sovereign intended to create a gallery in the Palazzo dei Regi Studi, a seventeenth-century building (and the present site of the Museo Archeologico in Naples), where he would bring together antiquities from Herculaneum and Pompeii and his collection of archaeological finds still kept in the Palazzo Farnese in Rome.

This plan was abruptly interrupted by the arrival in 1806 of the Napoleonic troops and the transfer, once again, of the royal family to Palermo. Under Joseph Bonaparte and Joachim Murat, work was resumed and expanded, with the acquisition of numerous paintings from monasteries that had been shut down in Naples and throughout the south. This was a result of new regulations promulgated by the French during their decade of rule, which called for the expropriation of Church assets. During this period the Capodimonte palace was inhabited by the French court, and renovation work resumed, with particular attention given to furnishings and furniture brought in directly from France. In 1815 Ferdinand returned from Sicily, having newly assumed the title of King of the Two Sicilies, and, with the Bourbon Restoration, important work on the palazzo was completed. Most importantly, the transfer of the art collections to the Palazzo dei Regi Studi was completed, thus creating the royal Museo Borbonico. Under the direction of royal architect Tommaso Giordano and the supervision of Antonio Niccolini, a Tuscan, the third courtyard and main staircase were finally completed, as was the hexagonal staircase in the south part of the building, in 1832. At the same time interior decorative work was carried out in the rooms set aside for official functions, with fireplaces designed by Niccolini and bronze candelabra created by the well-known Neapolitan sculptor Tito Angelini.

With the passage from the Bourbon to the Savoy dynasty (1860), the palazzo continued to be used as a royal residence. For nearly twenty years the administration of the household was entrusted to Annibale Sacco, who reorganized the collections, going back to the old Bourbon plan to construct a gallery of modern art on the *piano nobile*. For this reason, beginning in 1864 and depending on painters Domenico Morelli and Federico Maldarelli as advisors, he acquired numerous works by contemporary Neapolitan artists, which were added to works already present in this and other Bourbon palaces. Thus the collection gradually grew, further enriched by bequests and gifts. In 1864 the Bourbon collection of arms, including Farnese and Bourbon armor and weapons, was transferred from the Palazzo Reale. In 1866 the famous room of Chinese porcelain was shipped from the palace in Portici, which had been taken over by the state. This collection, which had belonged to Queen Maria Amalia of Saxony, consists of refined masterpieces of the genre, made in the factory set up by Charles III. In 1877 Roman marble pavement, discovered during the excavations of a villa in Capri, were placed in the "cradle room." Porcelain and ceramics that Annibale Sacco located in residences that had once belonged to the Bourbons further enriched the collection, along with tapestries made in Naples and numerous crèche figures.

But with the death of Sacco, the plan to create a museum at Capodimonte was set aside, and the palace was used exclusively as a royal residence. Victor Emmanuel II moved there when he acceded to the throne, and

preceding pages, left
Titian, *Paul III with his Nephews*, c. 1545.

preceding pages, right
Artemisia Gentileschi, *Judith and Holofernes*, 1625-30.

Sala della Culla ("cradle room"), marble floor from the Roman era, from a villa on Capri.

from 1906 onward it became the permanent residence of the family of the dukes of Aosta. They continued to live there until after the Second World War, even when, in 1920, the palazzo became state property and the Fine Arts Administration was charged with restoring it to its previous use as a museum.

After one of the most dramatic periods in the museum's history, during which the collection was dispersed as a result of plundering, transfers, and claims, a new and more rational approach was taken to the artistic legacy of the museums of Naples. In May 1949 the Palazzo di Capodimonte was chosen as the new location for the Pinacoteca, which was meant to include all the works in the collection of the Museo Borbonico, already in the Palazzo dei Regi Studi. The Museo Borbonico was then set aside to exclusively house collections of antiquities, and it was renamed the Museo Archeologico Nazionale.

Between 1952 and 1957 architect Ezio Bruno De Felice, under the supervision of Superintendent Bruno Molajoli, conducted extensive restoration work, which involved the rebuilding of the roofs, with reinforced concrete trusses and tie-beams in prestressed concrete. The pitch of the roofs was restored to their original angle, but since for technical reasons they were tied to the storm drains and to the ventilation screens, they were positioned fifty centimeters higher. Tempered glass screens of various sizes were placed on the roof, larger at the intersections of the slopes and above the exhibition spaces, smaller over the warehouses. The screens were made in various sizes and in different shapes, depending on the interior distribution of space and on exhibition requirements.

With a system of moveable fins arranged below the tilted skylights, there was a mechanism to regulate natural light. Access for inspecting the fins was also installed, along with a facility for water-cooled air, to avoid the effects of excessive overheating. The fourth-floor rooms are completely innovative in terms of quality of illumination and the spaces, and the museum is considered one of the finest exhibition facilities in Europe.

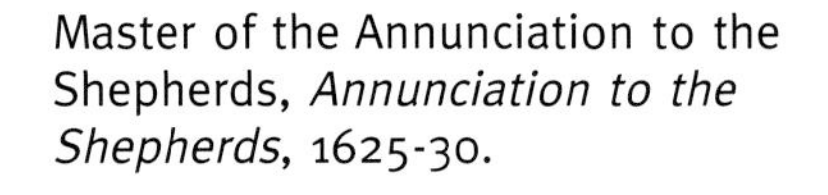

Master of the Annunciation to the Shepherds, *Annunciation to the Shepherds*, 1625-30.

Since the late 1970s Capodimonte has been the site of prestigious art exhibitions and important cultural events. The overall renovation and restoration plan, which has involved the entire complex, and the reorganization of the collections are nearing completion in 1999. The museum's collection of prints and drawings, which is particularly extensive and significant, was reorganized in 1995, as was the entire *piano nobile*, which includes the royal apartments. The east side houses a chronological exhibition of significant items from the Bourbon period, while the rooms located on the southwest side contain paintings and objects from the Farnese collection, ranging from Titian to Parmigianino, Correggio, and Caracci. There is also Cardinal Stefano Borgia's well-known collection, as well as valuable works acquired during the Bourbon and post-unification eras, which include a *Crucifixion* by Masaccio.

The third floor houses the most significant examples of Neapolitan art from the late thirteenth to the late eighteenth century. There are more than three hundred works, paintings and sculptures, from Bourbon and post-unification sources, including panels by Simone Martini, Colantonio, and Giorgio Vasari, Caravaggio's famous *Flagellation*, paintings by Battistello Caracciolo, Ribera, Cavallino, Luca Giordano, Francesco Solimena, Gaspare Traversi, Giuseppe Bonito, and Francesco de Mura.

Finally, there is a collection of contemporary art, located on the fourth floor of the museum, with a significant group of works created specifically for Capodimonte by internationally renowned artists.

Tommaso Solari, *Omphale*, life-size marble sculpture, formerly part of the furnishings of the royal residence, mid-19th century.

Michelangelo Merisi, known as Caravaggio, *Flagellation of Christ*, 1607/1609-10.

Reggia di Portici
(Royal Palace at Portici)

The royal palace of Portici was built during a period when the Bourbons were focusing new attention on the area around Vesuvius, due to archaeological discoveries that led to the excavations at Pompeii and Herculaneum, the ancient Roman cities buried by the eruption of A.D. 79. During this period the scenic qualities of the area were also taken into new consideration. According to Carlo Celano, during an excursion at sea to witness tuna fishing, the royals encountered a storm. The queen, struck by the beauty of the site, expressed a desire to create a residence outside the city but easily accessible, in an area where there were already some country villas. In reality, there were other motivations. King Charles did not care for Naples, and from the beginning of his reign, he planned to create residences outside the city where he could create a habitat more suitable for his own needs, which included a grand passion for hunting. This was the genesis of his plans for Capodimonte, Caserta, and Portici.

As Arnaldo Venditti and Cardarelli have pointed out,

The facade facing out toward the sea.

NIHIL EX NIHILO

The fortification for military drills, known as the "Castello," within the "Upper Woods," the present-day Parco Gussone.

the tendency to create residential dwellings outside the city, buildings not suited to the urban spaces of the metropolis, began in the sixteenth century, with the construction of Hampton Court, near London. The practice became widespread throughout Europe, with the building of the Escorial near Madrid (1563), Versailles near Paris (1661), Nymphenburg near Munich (1664), and Charlottenburg near Berlin (1695). Thus, compared to the rest of Europe, the phenomenon was late reaching Naples.

The site chosen by the king for the new palace was on the border between Portici and Resina and was occupied by the villas of the count of Palena, the prince of Santobuono, and the prince of Caramanico. The area also boasted the Palazzo Mascabruno and, on the sea, a villa built in 1711 by Ferdinando Sanfelice for Maurizio Emanuele di Lorena, prince of Elboeuf. The latter had initiated the excavations at Herculaneum, and his villa had become a repository for his statues and archaeological finds.

Between 1738 and 1742 the king acquired all the villas that occupied the land where his future palace would be built. Work began in 1738, with the adaptation of preexisting structures to the new plan. The court temporarily moved into the villa of the count of Palena. The design was first assigned to royal engineer Giovanni Antonio Medrano. Then, in 1741, it was turned over to Antonio Canevari, after Medrano became involved in a financial scandal. There were strong contrasts between the two men's approaches. Canevari, while still involved with Medrano, was also working on the palace of Capodimonte. These were not architecturally significant projects, nor were the facades for the churches of San Francesco and Sant'Eustachio, designed by Canevari in Rome, where he employed a conventional use of Baroque forms. The Portici palace was the most important and demanding project of Canevari's career. The new construction's configuration was unlike that of the numerous villas in the vicinity of Vesuvius. Most of these were located along the so-called "golden mile," the royal street that ran from Naples to Calbrie, parallel to the coast and crossing through San Giovanni a Teduccio, San Giorgio a Cremano, Portici, Herculaneum, Barra, and other Vesuvian towns. In contrast, most of the noble residences outside the city faced onto the road, with the back of the building open to the landscape. The palace sat astride the same road, its rectangular courtyard crossing it, creating a convergence of architecture and setting.

The entire design is articulated along two axes at right angles to each other.

One axis is the street, which changes direction slightly at the courtyard. The other axis passes through the deep porticoes with three barrel vaults on the two facades of each of the long building elements that flank the courtyard. One side faces Vesuvius, the other the sea. This layout in a certain sense defined the architectural characteristics of the mediocre facades—neither of which can be considered the main facade—positioned tangentially with a lack of strong projecting elements or complex decorative motifs. Giancarlo Alisio noted that in this same courtyard there seems to be an attempt to shape a sort of *place royale*, although within a very different context.

The most important eighteenth-century buildings of the Bourbon period often take into consideration the urban setting. Interiors are always conceived in relationship to the broader environmental context and, in particular, in terms of the perspectival axes that determine the architecture. In the palace at Caserta, Luigi Vanvitelli organized the building as a function of the rectilinear view from the tree-lined avenue to the waterfall, and he designed the courtyards as spaces of passage. As in Caserta, the courtyard in Portici has rounded corners, thus eliminating abrupt transitions in the interior facades, in an ideal expansion of the space to the open sky.

As Alisio has noted, the layout of the palace in Portici is also based on a desire to preserve the structure of the Palazzo Caramanico in the facade facing the sea and, on the other side, the count of Palena's garden. The facade facing the garden was rotated slightly in order to preserve the orthogonal relationship to the green area

The "Upper Garden," now the Botanical Garden of the School of Agriculture of the University of Naples Federico II.

The chapel in the Castello courtyard.

The Royal Staircase, with "faux architecture" frescoed by Vincenzo Re.

opposite. The gardens, which play an important role in the overall scheme, were designed by Francesco Geri and based on French models that were widespread throughout Europe, after André Le Nôtre's design for Louis XIV in Versailles. Thus from the beginning King Charles asked Medrano "for the garden of his Villa in Portici to have a French-style parterre."

In addition to the idea of an infinite perspective, the architecture also needed to be emphasized, and this entailed the elimination of the preexisting woods between the two long terraces that stretched out toward the sea. The garden vegetation to the sides of these terraces then was kept at a low height. At the back, toward the mountain, tile and stone paving led into the garden, where there was a fountain by Canart, with a base of fauna supporting an ancient statue of Flora. Beyond this garden there were woods scattered with court "pleasures." These included a space for performances with tiers of seats for spectators; an enclosure for ball playing, built for Ferdinand IV; a fortified piazza, built in 1775, where Charles's son organized military maneuvers, and where there also was a small chapel and an observatory; and a hermitage, a pheasantry, and a zoo for wild beasts.

As in Caserta, arrangements also had to be made for new fixtures and services, again in the context of the setting. The springs of Santa Maria a Pugliano, which Medrano had used for bringing water into the building, were not sufficient, and Luigi Vanvitelli and Ferdinando Fuga were brought in as consultants.

The ground floor of the palace on the side toward Vesuvius was taken up with service spaces. The side facing the sea housed the princes' apartments. The second floor was entirely taken up by the royal apartment, which was entered by two main staircases, located in two facing porticoes. Beneath the viaduct on the northwest side toward the mountain, there is a perfectly preserved chapel, accessible through a portal flanked by pairs of columns with two marble angels holding the royal coat of arms. Medrano's plan had called for an elliptical space with eight altars alternating with niches, surmounted by a tall, segmented dome. Instead, there is an initial, octagonal space with a pavilion roof, which leads, through a depressed arch, to a rectangular space with an imposing altar. The specific layout of the chapel derives from the fact that the space was originally conceived for a theater. The decorative program exhibits a clear contrast between the festoons that run around the entire space beneath the trabeation, the polychrome marble of the altars, the gilded wooden inlay of the women's gallery and the stage—all typically Baroque elements—and the neoclassical style of the white walls punctuated by pilasters with Ionic capitals.

Little remains of the eighteenth-century decorative schemes and paintings created during the construction of the villa. On the walls of the staircase in the wing overlooking the sea and in the two antechambers on the second floor on the same side of the building there are faux architectural elements, painted by Vincenzo Re. The ceilings of these second-floor spaces are decorated with *Truth Revealed by Time* and *Allegory of Dawn* by Crescenzo Gamba. The third reception hall, in very poor condition, still has a fresco depicting *The Meeting of the Gods*, painted by Gamba in 1750, surrounded by a decorative scheme by Vincenzo Re, which is better preserved. Giuseppe Bonito created a fresco of *The Visitation*, in the vault of the private chapel, the only example of his work in the palace.

Another room from the eighteenth-century, the "gold room," was decorated by Clemente Ruta with gilded stuccowork against a white ground. The "Chinese room" has scenes of Asian life within a *chinoiserie* setting that also prevails in the "gabinetto di porcellana," or porcelain room. The latter space was characterized by white porcelain finishings on the

walls and furnishings, with rich, orientalizing floral motifs. It was created by Stefano and Giuseppe Gricc and by the painter Johann Sigismund Fisher, and then, after Fisher's death, by Luigi Restile. The work was produced between 1757 and 1759 in the royal factory of Capodimonte which, in 1759, was moved to Spain by King Charles, on the occasion of his departure from Naples for his coronation. Ferdinand IV reopened the factory in 1771 in Portici, and it was later moved to the Palazzo Reale in Naples.

Archaeological finds from the excavations in Herculaneum, which Charles III had installed in the Palazzo Caramanico, played an important role in the furnishings, both inside and outside the palace. The Palazzo Caramanico was a veritable museum, its ground floor filled with objects (marble, glasswork, tools, bronzes, terracottas, and lamps), and paintings on the second floor.

The Royal Staircase, with "faux architecture" frescoed by Vincenzo Re, seen from a "viewing point" indicated on the floor, the optimum position for appreciating the illusionistic perspective of the pictorial space.

following page
"Sala della Guardia del Corpo" (royal guard room).

With the coming of the French, interior renovations were carried out from 1806 to 1814. This altered almost all the spaces of the palace and gave it a tone more in keeping with a private residence, doing away with the more public and official functions of the previous period. As Luisa Martorelli has stressed, the moderni-zation of the Portici palace bears the mark of Murat's neoclassical style; the work at Portici needs to be differentiated from contem-porary alterations at the Caserta palace—also by Giovanni Patturelli and Gennaro Bisogni—which was much more ceremonial in nature. In Portici the reorganization of the space was carried out according to a design by a Parisian architect-decorator, Etienne Cherubin Lecomte.

There are still obvious traces of this cultural climate, which was, for the most part, annulled during the restor-ation under Ferdinand. Many elements are comparable to the rooms of the queen's apartment, located on the southwest side of the palace, toward the sea. Martorelli's study points out that in early documents (1812), this large rectangular space is indicated as a "salone in Seguito," or a continuation of a reception hall. Later (1819) it is referred to as the "galleria Celeste," or celestial or sky-blue gallery, and finally (during the time of Pius IX's residence), in 1849, as an "audience chamber." Along with Bourbon Restoration period decorations, there are motifs from Murat's era, which, in turn, had eliminated a fresco by Giuseppe Bonito, *The Story of Bacchus*. Above the cornice, two hippogriffs raise their hooves onto ornamental plant motifs, painted to replace a globe from the French epoch. The figures are framed between continuous bands of acanthus leaves. On the ceiling one can still detect the pattern of gilded lozenge shapes that framed "alternating ears of corn and stars," later covered up by a blue ground with bands of corn ears alternating sideways with gilded stars. One can still see six *Sirens* and the monochrome figures of *Minerva, Mars, and Giustina*, which interrupt the background, framed by two candelabra. For the most part, the hall is characterized by the neoclassical vocabulary that followed the French period and can be ascribed to Bourbon taste.

Other elements, such as the initials "G" and "C" (referring to Joachim and Caroline Murat), can be found within the crown of laurel, at the center of two rooms that precede the Galleria Celeste. In the latter, a wooden partition delimits a small study with a mosaic floor. Above the cornice, a decorative gold band against a blue ground surrounds an eagle on a head, symbol of the French emperor. Above the crown, is *The Collar of Joachim Murat*, with fifteen

medallions surrounded by crowns of laurel, each with the coat of arms of a region in the kingdom.

There are also two frescoes of surprising illusionistic effect, heightened by their chromatic delicacy and by the overall composition. One covers a small space adjacent to the Galleria Celeste. A large transparent umbrella is painted on the ceiling with grotesque decorative motifs in neoclassical style, connected to the lunettes below by elegant linear motifs. The other ceiling is in a study located near the so-called Eating Hall, which is a result of the renovation of a preexisting, much larger eighteenth-century room covered with a cavetto vault, which is still visible. The ceiling of the study, covered with canvas, depicts a decorative trompe-l'oeil curtain that illusionistically expands the space.

In the scaled-down spaces of the palace, the French also installed a library of approximately two hundred volumes, called the *Petite bibliothèque* or the *Bibliothèque de S.M. la Reine des Deux Sicilies*. It contained many historical volumes on the Napoleonic empire and a lesser number of literary, scientific, and theater texts. During the French era, a series of works celebrating the Napoleonic dynasty were installed—paintings by P. E. Martin; F. Gerard, and Costanzo Angelini. Along with these, there were other paintings by Auguste de Forbin and François Maria Granet, modern artists who had trained in the style of David, attesting to Caroline Murat's interest in new developments in French figurative art.

With the Bourbon restoration, many signs of the previous period were annulled, for obvious political reasons. The paintings in the Murat collection were also temporarily placed in storage, but were reconsidered in 1823, when the Bourbon dynasty expressed renewed interest in them. This formed the genesis of Ferdinand's collection. An inventory of the palace conducted in 1835 confirms this new regard for the French pictorial legacy, which also is reflected in the smaller paintings in *troubadour* style (with references to neo-Gothic and medieval

preceding page
"Sala della Guardia del Corpo," ceiling frescoes by Crescenzo Gamba, *Truth Revealed by Time*, with allegorical figures, mid-18th century.

Chinoiserie decoration by Antonio Cipullo, in the "billiard room."

themes), executed by young painters, both local and foreign, such as Giovanni Cobianchi, Salvatore Fergola, and Louis Nicolas Lemasle.

Meanwhile, in 1822, the collection of items from Herculaneum was moved to Naples, depriving the building of one of its specific roles, tied to the exhibition of archaeological finds, which was linked to the site and the reasons for its very conception and construction. This loss of significance was followed by the gradual removal of ancient pieces that ornamented the architecture itself.

In 1860 the palace became the property of the state, and the complex was divided. The Palazzo Mascabruno was turned into a barracks. In 1872, when much of the main core of the former palace was acquired by the Regional Administration of Naples, the Agricultural Institute was located there. Today both the building and the surrounding park are the site of the School of Agriculture of the University of Naples.

Detail of the *chinoiserie* decoration of the "billiard room."

Decorative detail with allegorical figures and gilded, carved frame, 18th century.

Albergo dei Poveri
(Poorhouse)

The construction of the Albergo dei Poveri in Naples began in the mid-eighteenth century. Its connotations are numerous, and it expresses both the development of the city and the paternalistic policies of the Bourbons toward their subjects, tied to the very concept of political power at that time. For centuries, the concept of "charity" had connoted Neapolitan society and, consequently, the shape and development of the city.

Beginning in the first half of the sixteenth century, there was a noticeable increase in the number of monasteries, hospitals and welfare centers, often tied to religious orders. These involved the creation of a multiplicity of monastery *insulae* within the urban setting, institutions that carried out widespread programs of charity.

The creation of the Albergo dei Poveri, while directed toward analogous goals, such as assistance to the poor and needy, was, however, quite different. It was a plan for "centralized charity," adhering to precise criteria of isolation and confinement of the needy, similar to ideas advanced previously in the regulation of the Ospizio di San Gennaro dei Poveri in 1671. As Andrea Guerra has noted, that institution represented an attempt to adjust an existing monastic structure to the hygienic and moral rules of reclusion.

But while the Albergo dei Poveri was an organized structure in response to needs for control, the "widespread charity" through monasteries in the old city responded to the need for these institutions to acquire power through the exercise of a precise role within the urban community. In other words, this was a specific product of royal power, "external" to the poorhouse. In this building, the ruling authorities found a tool for

G. Galli, *View of the Royal Poorhouse*, gouache (Naples, San Martino Museum).

Drawing by Ferdinando Fuga of the ground floor for the definitive project.

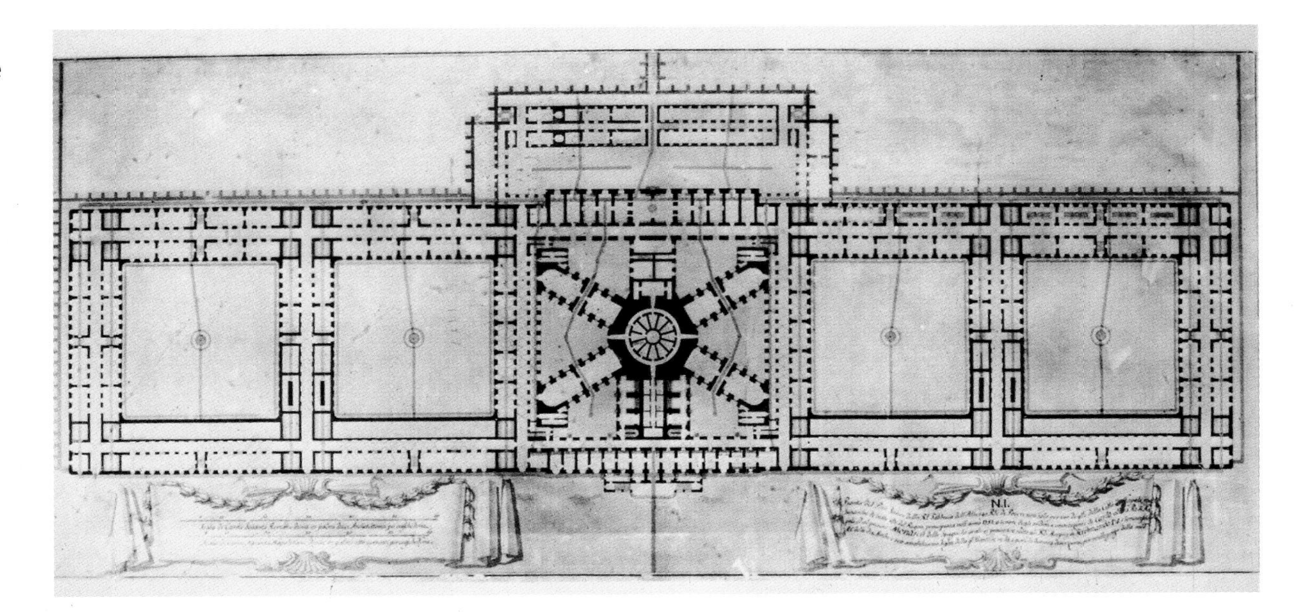

below and opposite
View of the building block of the central church (unfinished), with four radiating naves (also unfinished), set aside for the "inmates."

Access stairs from Via Foria.

regulating the existence of an entire category of subjects. In earlier instances, power was internal to the monasteries, hospitals, and charitable institutions and was identified as a direct function of charitable assistance.

The idea of constructing the new, enormous structure also involved a desire to give work to the needy, transforming an unemployed segment of the population into a concrete tool of production. There were plans for raw materials from the hinterlands, such as wool, silk, and hemp, to be worked by the "residents," transformed into manufactured goods, and exported by ship outside the kingdom.

This economic concept, French in derivation, was substantially innovative, in that it was based on free trade through the movement of goods. During the period of the Spanish and Austrian viceroys, Naples had been the exclusive end point of a process of immigration, with consequent and growing imbalances in the social and economic order.

In the realization of this program, however, the initial production component gave way to the need to control a substantial portion of the population, for the most part unemployed and thus a potential source of unrest. The church played a role in this change of perspective, as Andrea Guerra has pointed out. This is confirmed in a letter dated 24 August 1748, from Gualtieri, papal envoy to Naples, to Cardinal Valenti Gonzaga, about the proposal for the large Albergo dei Poveri put forth by the Domenican father Gregorio Maria Rocco.

In August 1748 a commission made up of three doctors and a single architect, Antonio Canevari, was established to choose the site. For a project of this scale, representative of the new dynasty, it was necessary to turn to a personality who could play a leading role in all phases of the process, from initial concept to final completion of the building. The project was assigned to Roman architect Ferdinando Fuga, a figure substantially absent from Neapolitan circles. In 1736 Fuga had been named royal architect by Charles III Bourbon, and he had carried out various assignments, accumulating a prestigious resume that probably worked to his advantage in obtaining the commission.

Initially the Albergo was to have been built in the Loreto district, aligned along the Santa Maria di Loreto road and creating a new road network, with a Via Arenaccia detour. Fuga's design presented a square plan with two interior cross-shaped wings, which delineated four courtyards. This echoed a scheme adopted by Vanvitelli for the Caserta palace, which, in its turn, had been inspired by a Roman palazzo for a religious group, built by Filippo Juvarra in 1725. This latter building was planned with the isolation and self-sufficiency of the prelates in mind—characteristics that were analogous to the basic criteria for Fuga's building. The design was later changed, however, without altering the form and position of the refectory and kitchen, placed at the back, and the church, located at the middle of the front facade, at the point of intersection with an intermediary wing. This arrangement is different from one planned by Scaniglia for a hospice in Genoa, where the church is placed at the intersection of the interior wings.

Thus the facade of the church was placed at the center of the front elevation. It had a single colossal order, placed atop a tall base, and a large dome on a tall drum. The housing for the bells is indicated with small domes to the right and left, giving maximum emphasis to the central dome. The elevation of the church constitutes the only prominent element in the facade, which has uninterrupted series of windows in four rows, with an intermediary stringcourse and the ends punctuated by four gigantic pilasters in a double row, corresponding to the ends of the side wings. In this first concept, which was not built, the church and the refectories were removed too far from the general distribution of the elements and placed in the more distant areas of the complex, although it made sense from a symbolic standpoint. The other two external side elements corresponded to laboratories and dormitories, so that the four elevations were an expression of the distributive and functional program within.

It is not known precisely why the project was abandoned, but probably—as Roberto Pane has indicated—the military nature of the area, in the end, made the Loreto district an ill-advised choice. Indeed, the area boasted the Castello del Carmine, the large barracks that Vanvitelli built at the end of the district, and the Granili, used as a military barracks and depot. All these were in the vicinity of the port.

A new area was identified, along the Via del Campo, the most important road connecting to the hinterland, at the foot of the Capodimonte hill. The geography of the area did not allow the square format of the previous design. The new design had five elongated courtyards, with a church in the central one. If fully built, this would have been six hundred meters long and ten thousand square meters larger than the first solution, with a greater number of laboratories, workshops and dormitories.

Andrea Guerra has compared the layout of the new plan—construction of which began between 1750 and 1751—to the hospital in Lyons by Jacques-Germain Soufflot, both in the configuration of the plan and in the symbolism. This can be seen in the principal facade, where, in correspondence to the central portion, the entrance is characterized by three round arches, approached from an exterior gallery connected at street level by a symmetrical double flight of steps clad in travertine. The central coping consists of a triangular tympanum. The long facade, reduced by the elimination of the two end courtyards, is divided horizontally by two stringcourse bands. The lower band, at the level of the entrance gallery, defines the dark base against which the staircase body stands out.

Unfinished interior facade.

The central part, considerably extended, is punctuated by large pilasters that repeat, corresponding to the ends of the side closings.

Along the immense facade are rows of windows, outlined by smooth squares. The lack of decorative or projecting elements is due, not only to economic factors, but also to the location of the building along the Via del Campo, from which it could be seen only at an angle. The later imposition of a trident of late-nineteenth-century streets completely distorted the relationship of the architecture to its immediate setting.

The central courtyard was meant to contain a church, the hexagonal layout of which can be discerned from projections emerging from the walls. It would have had eight altars, six along the sides, a seventh at the center, and an eighth set back along the transverse axis opposite the entrance.

The dome would no longer have been a dominating architectural motif on the principal facade, since it was moved back to the center of the intermediary courtyard. The center of the facade consisted of a triangular tympanum. Inside, hallways led to the central portion of the long building elements, with rooms to the right and left. The spaces were covered with barrel vaults, interrupted by groins or by cloister vaults, with consequent varied effects of lighting.

The entire project, which was never completed, represented a new development for the city, both in its elongated form and in its urban position. It needs to be considered within the framework of Bourbon projects executed on a vast urban scale.

Unfinished interior structures.

Entrance vestibule from Piazza Carlo III.

Villa Campolieto

The Vesuvian villas constitute a group of residences outside the city that were built within a twenty-year period, from 1745 to 1765, in the area between San Giovanni a Teduccio, Portici, Resina (now Herculaneum), and Torre del Greco. They were built after the creation of the Portici palace, following a wave of interest in the discovery of Pompeii and Herculaneum, subsequent to the excavations begun by the prince of Elboeuf. But the area was already known for various villas, some of which date back to the eleventh through thirteenth centuries. The area around Vesuvius had always been considered desirable on account of the exceptional richness of its soil, which was cultivated with fruit trees, vineyards, and mulberry trees, particularly beginning in the eighteenth century. During this period there were not many "pleasure gardens," and the region was characterized by well-ordered fields of crops. Buildings were more like farm complexes than suburban villas. During the eighteenth century, the farms prospered, and many people began to emulate the worldly style they saw at the Portici palace. A different type of construction appeared, with a courtly sense of space, enriched by the landscape attributes of the site. The development of open spaces and parkland also dates back to this time, in conjunction with a growth in botanical studies, a result of the new scientific interests of Enlightenment culture. Thus fields were increasingly transformed into gardens of exotic plants, integrated with "pleasure garden" architecture for the re-creation of families and guests. The interiors of the villas also were adapted to this new concept of use and space. More emphasis was given to formal, public spaces, with attention also paid to connecting spaces such as staircases, atriums, and terraces. These were organized along precise axes

Circular portico and "pincer-shaped" ramps on the facade looking out toward the sea.

following page
The facade looking out toward the sea from the circular portico.

and visual perspectives, oriented to the position of the villa. Private rooms and, in general, any features of domesticity, were treated with much less regard. Gradually these villas approached the scale of royal palaces. Sited along the royal road, they grew in number, concrete proof of the lure of the royal residence outside the city.

Excluding villas that basically were farms, tied to agricultural production—above all isolated farmhouses along the slopes of the volcano—the phenomenon was mostly one of so-called "gentlemen's" villas, aligned along the royal road or its branches. These had facades at the edge of the street, with the side wings often of the same height or lower. In contrast to the street facade, the building usually opened up to the landscape in the back. Thus the street side had an "urban" dimension, while the back had a "landscape" configuration.

Villa Campolieto, one of the most famous Vesuvian residences, has all these characteristics. It has an extremely balanced composition that, using Vanvitelli's vocabulary, expressed the most up-to-date architectural approach of the time. Don Luzio de' Sangro, duke of Casacalenda, commissioned architect Mario Gioffredo to design the building. The site, only a bit more than one kilometer from the royal palace, was purchased between 1755 and 1757. Work went on for

approximately twenty years because of the eruption of Vesuvius in 1758-59, as well as disputes between the duke and his neighbors and disagreements between client and architect, which arose during the construction of the Palazzo dei Casacalenda in Piazza San Domenico Maggiore in Naples. In 1760 Gioffredo withdrew from the project, and the work, temporarily directed by Michelangelo Giustiniani, slowed down for about three years. In 1763 Luigi Vanvitelli was hired. Gioffredo's design, based on the duke of Noja's plan, called for the facade to be stepped back about six meters from the royal road, with a sort of colonnade that would create a protected space for carriages arriving at the villa. When the villa was built, however, the main body was brought right to the edge of the road. The facade is divided into lower

preceding page
The circular terrace on the portico projecting out toward the sea.

North room with frescoes by Jacopo Cestaro and Gaetano and Giuseppe Magri.

West room with pergola frescoed by Fedele Fischetti.

and upper areas. The lower zone includes an arched portal and a series of rectangular openings on the ground floor, with small windows on the upper floor. Higher up, a row of tall windows surmounted by a triangular tympanum alternates with pairs of pilasters, interrupted at the center, on axis with the entrance below, by an arched window resting on two columns. Above the unremarkable cornice, the entire building is crowned by a continuous balustrade, alternating now and then with slender masonry piers.

The entrance is through a hall covered with a barrel vault, from which, along the longitudinal axis directed toward the sea, one moves into an elongated vestibule. This space is illuminated from the right, where, as in Caserta, the staircase is arranged along the opposite side, so as to not interrupt the view. Both here and in Caserta, the staircase has a central ramp and two side ramps that lead to the light-filled space of the floor above, which is covered by a tall dome. The vestibule leads, through a vaulted passage analogous to the entrance hall, to an external horseshoe-shaped colonnade with a terrace above. Further along, a double "pincer-shaped" ramp descends to the garden. Two straight ramps arranged symmetrically against the rear facade connect the curved terrace atop the colonnade

preceding pages, left
Detail of pergola frescoed by Fedele Fischetti in the west room, with the collaboration of decorative painters Gaetano and Giuseppe Magri. The figure has traditionally been recognized as a portrait of Vanvitelli.

preceding pages, right
Staircase leading to the upper floors.

Detail of frescoes by Jacopo Cestaro and Gaetano and Giuseppe Magri in the north room.

Vestibule on the *piano nobile*.

to a balcony-level terrace. Through this controlled play of volumes to be negotiated, Luigi Vanvitelli effectively tied the main body of the villa to the setting, heightening the design overall through the theatrical device of the colonnade. In 1770 Vanvitelli called upon the usual painters with whom he worked—Fedele Fischetti and Jacopo Cestaro—to collaborate on the decoration of the interior spaces. Vanvitelli himself defined the entire decorative program. Fischetti had already worked on the Palazzo dei Casacalenda in Naples. In one of the spaces, he painted a pergola on the walls, with vines and climbing plants amid statues, cherubs, and cavaliers. He thus transformed the interior into an illusory space that referred to both the function and the location of this out-of-town dwelling and, as Spinosa noted, defined "a suggestive if fictitious continuity between interior and exterior space." In the other rooms, such as, for example, the south hall, Fischetti painted allegorical scenes amid faux architecture. Some frescoes, such as the *Scenes from the Life of Alexander* and the *Dream of Alexander*, were removed in 1922 and 1956 respectively, and transferred to the Museo di Capodimonte.

Jacopo Cestaro decorated three rooms, depicting *Apollo*, *Aurora*, and *Cupid* with putti in flight, amid faux colonnades. The

painted architectural structures, clearly derived from Luigi Vanvitelli's ideas and directions, were created by decorators Giuseppe and Gaetano Magri. There is almost no documentation about the work of Crescenzo Gamba, who was also called in to work on the interior decoration.

preceding page
The frescoed dome of the vestibule on the *piano nobile*.

Pictorial decoration of the ceiling of a room on the second floor.

Palazzo Casacalenda

Facade facing Piazza San Domenico Maggiore.

Reception hall, first *piano nobile*.

following page
Fedele Fischetti, *Allegory of Jupiter on Olympus*, ceiling decoration of the reception hall on the first *piano nobile*, second half of the 18th century.

In 1754 Marianna de' Sangro, duchess of Casacalenda, entrusted Mario Gioffredo with the task of preparing a renovation plan for her property in Piazza San Domenico Maggiore.

Initially the plan called for a general restoration of the old existing palazzo, leaving intact a staircase by Cosimo Fanzago and renovating the stucco-clad facade. The plan also called for the expansion of the building, to accommodate the service areas of the church of Santa Maria della Rotonda and the area beyond the Vicolo Pallonetto a Santa Chiara, occupied by the house of Duke Borgia. The latter opportunity fell through, and the Duchess focused on a different plan, which concentrated the building volumes in the area occupied by her own palazzo, enlarging only the side near the church.

Giuseppe Fiengo has pointed out that Gioffredo's plan was made up of twenty-seven panels, unfortunately now dispersed, where the initial solutions and later modifications were represented. The project as planned would have entailed not only a different structural layout and distribution of spaces, but also a complete renovation of the elevations, re-covered in "stone, and designed with the necessary divisions."

During construction, Greek walls from the fourth century B.C. were discovered. They would have descended from the gate of the city, corresponding to the piazza, down the Via Mezzocannone. In accordance with a customary practice of the time, Gioffredo did not hesitate to reutilize the material he discovered below ground. Cosimo Fanzago's staircase was also torn down, even though the duchess appreciated its importance.

Gioffredo continued working until 1761, when he realized that Marianna de' Sangro, who had initiated a lawsuit against master builder Donato Cosentino, also intended to sever the professional relationship that governed his services. According to Fiengo's detailed study, from 1754 to 1761 the architect attempted to receive payment from the duchess for his entire bill. Thus began an extremely long dispute, closely linked

Fedele Fischetti, *Winged Spirit*, detail of the ceiling decoration of the reception hall on the first *piano nobile*, second half of the 18th century.

Detail, border decoration for the reception hall ceiling, first *piano nobile*.

to the progress of work. Expert opinions were requested from various technicians and designer-surveyors, including architect Giuseppe Astarita and engineer Carlo Zoccoli, who for a certain period had also carried out some work. Gaetano de Tommaso, Giovanni d'Alessandro, Leonardo Carelli, and finally Michelangelo Porzio were brought in to help determine the size of the lot. The number of people involved in the initial phase (and those mentioned here are only a few) give an idea of the intensity of the dispute, which dragged on until the early years of the new century, involving the daughters of the architect and the heirs of the duchess. Although Gioffredo's claims were finally recognized, the long dispute did not help his professional activity, undermined both by suspicions aroused by the accusations against him and by the contemporary activity of Vanvitelli, who had replaced Michelangelo Giustiniani in July 1762 (Giustiniani had been brought in to replace Gioffredo). Vanvitelli blamed the designer and director of works for construction flaws that were detected, particularly along the side of the Via Mezzocannone. He discovered enormous damage where the construction attached to the church of Santa Maria della Rotonda, at the corner between Piazza San Domenico Maggiore and Via Mezzocannone. In June 1763 Alberto de Pompeis was assigned to the problem, along with trustworthy experts hired by both parties.

The church suffered considerable damage in 1845, when the palazzo was subdivided into numerous properties. It was torn down in 1922 when the Via Mezzocannone was widened, eliminating the last corner bay of the building.

According to documentation, the palazzo should be attributed almost entirely to Mario Gioffredo, except for some work on the facade, where Vanvitelli redid the pilasters and the balconies, plastering over the original stone work.

In the eighteenth century the use of natural, exposed materials fell out of practice, in favor of a more widespread use of plaster. This was more economical (particularly in the execution of decorative details) and at the same time corresponded to a new taste, which sought a different type of harmony among the parts of a building, an approach that could be controlled and manipulated through the color and tone of the stucco.

In conclusion, the general structural configuration and distribution of the spaces can be attributed to Gioffredo, as well as the layout of the facade. Generally speaking, Vanvitelli's responsibilities were for the finishings and for bringing certain work to completion, both of which did affect the

final appearance of the building. The contributions of other professionals who worked on the site during the 1760s should not be excluded. Astarita in particular was probably responsible for the solution of the sloped flights of steps, at two corners, leading to the symmetrical ramps opposite, at the back of the courtyard.

The first story of the main facade overlooking Piazza San Domenico Maggiore is articulated by stone arcades edged in relief against an exposed brick wall, with a depressed arch on the ground level surmounted by a rectangular window.

On the *piano nobile*, balconies were placed between the giant plastered pilasters, against the areas of exposed brick. Moving from the bottom up, these are surmounted by alternating curved and triangular tympanums. Next come small intermediary square windows with a single window with wide bands, organically connected to the decorated supporting brackets of the balconies above. Then there are tall balcony openings, which reach as far as the fascia of the upper coping. Above, there is a projecting cornice with corbels in relief; an additional floor was added later, with small balconies interspersed with sections of

Chinoiserie on the ceiling of a room on the first *piano nobile*.

pilaster, continuing those below. Toward the end of the 1760s, the painter Fedele Fischetti, assisted by Giuseppe and Gaetano Magri, worked on the ornamental portions of the interior.

Fischetti's work, influenced by Batoni and Mengs in Rome, and to a lesser degree by de Mura and Bonito, evolved after the 1770s into late Baroque taste. He employed images of refined elegance, marked by a new tendency toward classicism and compositional rigor, typical of architects of the Roman school working in Naples, namely Fuga and Vanvitelli.

Fischetti worked in various parts of the palazzo. In two rooms on the third floor, known as the "Galleria," he executed three frescoes of the *Dream of Alexander*, which were detached and shipped to Capodimonte in 1922, when the wing on the Via Mezzocannone was torn down. According to Nicola Spinosa, these frescoes display a "still subtly *rocaille* taste."

The second floor, originally designed as a private apartment for the duke and duchess, contains the well-preserved *Allegory of Jupiter on Olympus*, also by Fischetti. There are two other incomplete frescoes: one, probably by Fischetti, exists in fragmentary condition; the other, by Crescenzo Gamba, is missing its central portion but seems to manifest a taste for *chinoiserie*.

The third floor was occupied by the Casacalenda family until 1831, then by the Del Balzo family.

Chinoiserie on the ceiling of a room on the first *piano nobile*.

Palazzo d'Angri

Principal facade on Largo dello Spirito Santo.

Hexagonal courtyard, with the remains of hanging walkways, built beginning in 1839.

following page
The sequence of spaces opening off the hexagonal courtyard.

One of the most exemplary buildings of the late eighteenth century, the palazzo looks out on the Largo dello Spirito Santo, its three-storied, monumental marble facade aligned with the trapezoidal block formed by the Via Toledo and the Via Sant'Anna dei Lombardi, which converge in front of its entrance.

An archway flanked by pairs of Doric columns leads to a sort of unexpected "gallery" that enlivens the building's interior through an alternation of light from the courtyards and shadow from the entrance halls. The gallery also allows more natural light to reach the interior spaces.

The building was erected in the space between the old Aragonese and vice-regency walls. Part of this area was called the "Bancomangiare," due to its past history as a location for pastry work-shops. It takes up a triangular lot, which can be seen in a bird's-eye view of the city by Lafréry, dated 1556. In that image, the terrain is still substantially free of structures and almost entirely covered with irregular vegetation, with a few low cottages and a chapel with a

Rooms of the noble apartment.

small bell tower between the Via Nilo and the Via Monteoliveto.

Building activity intensified along the Via Toledo, due to the construction of the new Palazzo Reale by Domenico Fontana, and at the beginning of the new century, free areas of land thus acquired increasing importance. New residences in the district became symbols of social status and were rapidly occupied, and existing buildings were expanded with additional floors. As a result, the city acquired a new face.

In 1629—the date of the first view of the city by Baratta—the lot was already occupied by two buildings, which were separated by a small street parallel to the Via Nilo, leading into the Via Toledo. The structure, stepped back from the Spirito Santo corner, is quite tall, with the main entrance opposite the palazzo acquired by the duke of Maddaloni. The two buildings, both constructed between the 1660s and 1680s, were similar to others being built in Naples at the time, with white facades and window reveals painted dark gray (or bardiglio gray), with numerous balconies and porch roofs, in keeping with local traditions.

The wall surfaces were predominantly stucco, considered a less costly material than stone or marble. On the ground floor there were numerous workshops for foodstuffs and entertainment for "foreigners."

Prince Marcantonio Doria purchased the larger palazzo in 1749 and the other one in 1755, with the idea of creating a more dignified structure that would also occupy the old vicolo separating the two buildings. In fact, he built a raised walkway, covered in wood, which joined the upper levels of the two palazzi, as seen in the plan of Naples of the duke of Noja, from 1775, where the old narrow street has been widened. Then, in place of the planned reconstruction, he carried out a series of interventions with the existing structures.

After Marcantonio's death, in 1760, work on the larger palazzo was continued by his son, Giovan Carlo Doria. Except for the construction of a new staircase and the opening of a formal entrance on the Via Toledo, these were essentially finishings and embellishments. During this period Ferdinando Fuga, who had been called to Naples by King Charles III, expressed interest in the building, both in overseeing the work in progress and in presenting a general and unified plan for renovation.

The construction of the new building entailed the complete demolition of the building overlooking the Largo dello Spirito Santo and the substantial rebuilding of the older, taller structure behind it. In addition to Fuga, the best architects working in Naples, from Mario Gioffredo to Luigi Vanvitelli and his son Carlo, were involved, although at different times.

The final configuration of the building is essentially the work of Carlo Vanvitelli, although now it is contended that the plan—with sketches, drawings, and perhaps also a model—was prepared under the supervision of his father, Luigi. When Luigi Vanvitelli died in 1773, Carlo took over the project.

The principal facade and monumental entrance were built on the Largo dello Spirito Santo. This design

took advantage of the ample space in front of the building, from which the architecture could be perceived as a whole—an unusual situation in a city like Naples, where exterior space is a rarity.

The facade is structured on three levels. The entrance, flanked by two pairs of Doric columns, is surmounted by a balcony, with a balustrade with small columns extending to the sides in relation to the windows. The vertical structures continue at the upper levels, denoted with pilasters and with two columns to the side of the large central window. As in most of Luigi Vanvitelli's work, a colossal order is not adopted; this the architect reserved for royal palaces. The overall style of the building fits between the late Baroque and the neoclassical, to which the clear, rational structure belongs, determined by the vertical structures and horizontal elements, without a predominance of strong chiaroscuro.

A second entrance on Via Toledo was originally planned but never built, and alternative access was located instead in the facade facing the Palazzo Maddaloni. The entire composition in plan is therefore articulated along a sort of longitudinal axis that links the two entrances through the entrance halls, with the circular and rectangular courtyards in turn united by an intermediary vaulted passageway: a veritable interior route, an alternative to the street outside. This is a version of the "telescope" scheme favored by Vanvitelli. At the palace in Caserta, he fully realized this scheme on a landscape, rather than on an architectural, scale. There, before the tree-lined avenue leading to the large piazza was cut by a railroad line, it was possible to visually take in the entire volume of the complex. One could look out along the axis of the gardens, arriving as far as the gleam of the artificial waterfall created at the end, on the mountain. That end point, rendered indistinct by the distant perspective and by the movement of the water, represented *architecturally* the concept of infinity, typical of eighteenth-century culture.

In the Palazzo d'Angri, the shape of the lot made it impossible to create a perfect axial relationship between the two entrances. Nevertheless, design elements strengthen this intention, from the position of the staircase to the pursuit of a

Details of the fresco in the "oval room."

following page
Fresco by Fedele Fischetti, Alessandro Fischetti, and Costantino Desiderio in the ceiling of the "oval room" on the *piano nobile*.

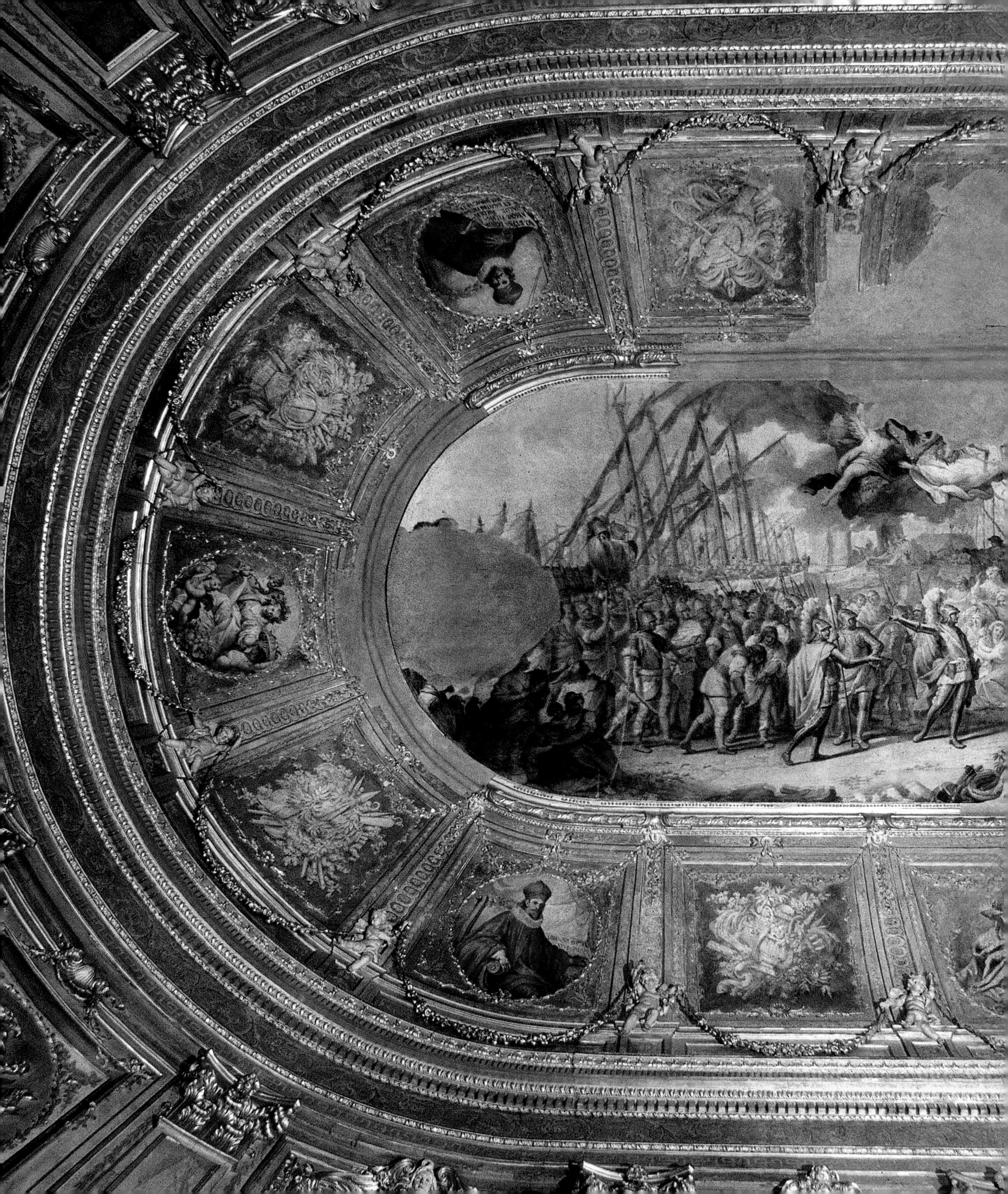

regular symmetry and the study of the light. All these were exploited in terms of the axial composition, which concluded beyond the Via Tommaso Senise, against the portal of Fanzago's Palazzo Maddaloni.

Numerous leading artists were engaged in the decorative scheme for the interior. Fedele Fischetti, along with Alessandro Fischetti and Costantino Desiderio, created the fresco for the vault of the large oval gallery. Fedele Fischetti also decorated six rooms of the "first noble quarter," overlooking the Via Toledo. Giacinto Diano frescoed the gallery and study in the "second noble quarter," the bedchamber of which was decorated by Girolamo Starace. Fischetti also hung three paintings by Francesco Solimena. Giovanni Maria Griffon painted an "oval on canvas" for the chapel on the *piano nobile*.

Later decorative and restoration work in the nineteenth century was directed by architect Antonio Francesconi. There were also later adaptations and modifications after the palazzo was divided into different dwellings, and hanging corridors were installed in the courtyards.

Detail of a fresco in a room on the *piano nobile*.

Villa Floridiana

The area now occupied by the Villa Floridiana was the property of Cristoforo Saliceti, a Minister of Police, before being inherited by his daughters Caterina and Angelica. On 20 September 1817 the vast lot, located on the Vomero hill, was acquired by Ferdinard I, king of the Two Sicilies (ruled earlier as Ferdinand IV, king of Naples). His first wife, Maria Carolina of Austria, had died, and he wanted to create a summer residence as a gift to his second wife, Lucia Migliaccio, whom he wed in a morganatic marriage (that is, without her receiving the title of queen). Lucia Migliaccio, duchess of Floridiana, was the widow of Benedetto Grifeo, prince of Partanna. The park, "La Floridiana," was named in her honor. Ferdinand also acquired a palazzo for her in Piazza Santa Caterina, the present Piazza dei Martiri, to be used as a winter residence, so that the duchess would not have to take up permanent residence in the Palazzo Reale, although the king arranged an apartment for her there as well.

The renovation of the property, which had a

The north facade with the main entrance.

The Belvedere tempietto.

"casino," now the Villa Floridiana, a coffee house, now the Villa Lucia, and a surrounding park, was entrusted by the king to a Tuscan architect, Antonio Niccolini. He had been brought to Naples in 1806 by Joseph Bonaparte, where he played a leading role, receiving the most important commissions tied to the royal family. In this complex, Niccolini succeeded in achieving a perfect balance between the elegant neoclassical buildings and the English-style layout of the park. Certain solutions are particularly charming, such as the Ionic tempietto, located on the far west slope, where it dominates the landscape below, or the area planted with camellia trees that create a multicolored carpet when they are in bloom. The little theater "della verdura" or "verzura" is also noteworthy. It is a sort of natural theater, elliptical in plan, raised up with trees acting as wings for the actors and the audience area made from stone steps surrounded by myrtle bushes. In general, the park was conceived in conformity with the concept of the English romantic garden, characterized by changes in terrain, winding avenues, dense areas of shade, steep cliffs, and unexpected picturesque vistas, where isolated architectural elements complete and embellish the natural setting. To fulfill the requirements of neoclassical taste, symmetrical plantings were placed close to the buildings.

For the main building, the architect substantially modified the structure that Saliceti had built, creating a villa with a symmetrical plan: a central rectangular element, two perpendicular wings, and a covered portico in front of the north entrance, for carriages. This architectural solution, which allowed people "to descend from carriages under cover" (as the plan, now in the Museo Nazionale di San Martino, reads in Niccolini's hand), is adopted from the San Carlo theater, rebuilt by the same architect. The south side of the building, where the land slopes so steeply that the basement level is exposed, has a base covered in lava stone, to which a marble staircase is attached, connecting the villa to the surrounding park and opening up a view of the city. The rich interior of the villa, which Niccolini personally supervised in terms of furnishings and decoration, is known through descriptions in contemporary sources.

What remains of this noble residence are one small room (where majolica from Castelli is exhibited), its stuccoed ceiling decorated with mythological figures and putti, and a large central reception hall on the upper floor. The latter room looks out northward toward the park and southward toward the sea. It is finely decorated in stuccowork and paintings,

in the taste of the time, with bas-reliefs depicting the Four Seasons above the doors, a frieze inlaid with lilies and with crowns of flowers in relief, and marble cornices and consoles surmounted by mirrors. The entire room is dominated by a vault with a painted sky and putti in flight, by Giuseppe Cammarano.

The preexisting staircase with three flights was replaced by the current, double-ramp staircase. The villa also contained a chapel, a billiard hall, and a new bathroom, all of which have disappeared over the successive changes in ownership. After the death of the duchess, the property was eventually divided among her children from her first marriage—Giuseppe, Luigi, and Marianna. The original plan, which, along with numerous original drawings, is in the Museo di San Martino, reflected the duchess of Floridiana's interests and called for cages and caves for tigers, lions, and bears, and an enclosure for kangaroos. Over time, however, the park, as laid out, has undergone numerous transformations. In the southern portion, the elliptical parterre was replaced by curved flower beds and avenues. The original staircase, with only four flights, was extended as far as the fountain, to highly theatrical effect. Finally, the long avenue that led to the

The south facade looking toward the sea.

following page
The panoramic view of the Belvedere tempietto.

villa from the Vomero street was interrupted halfway and replaced with a winding route, so that the villa would come into view unexpectedly.

In 1919 the villa was acquired by the Italian state to house an extraordinary collection of porcelain, majolica, glass, furniture, enamels, ivory, and other decorative art objects. These had been collected during the second half of the nineteenth century and then were donated to the city of Naples in 1911, by Placido de' Sangro, count of Marsi.

From 1927 onward, the palazzo has housed the Museo Nazionale della Ceramica Duca di Martina.

Groups in porcelain, made at the Fabbrica di Capodimonte del Buen Retiro; at the Center, *Three Putti with a Ram*, 1765-83.

Giuseppe Cammarano, *Flying Putti*, detail of the frescoes in the ceiling of the central reception hall, first half of the 19th century.

Villa Acton Pignatelli

The princely residence called the Villa Pignatelli, from the name of the last owners, is one of the most significant examples of neoclassical architecture in Naples.

The structure, surrounded by an ample park, is stepped back from the palazzi of the Riviera di Chiaia. It was built, beginning in 1826, by Pietro Valente, a young Neapolitan architect and pupil of Antonio Niccolini. The project was commissioned by the English baronet, Sir Ferdinand Acton.

In March 1826 Acton came into the possession of a vast terrain "with marshes" along the Riviera di Chiaia, surrounded by agricultural plots. A dwelling belonging to the Carafa family had been demolished earlier on this site. In 1825 the previous owner, Lord Drummond, had commissioned architect Giuseppe Giordano to design a building stepped back from the street, which was unusual in Naples. As Fabio Mangone has noted, work began between 1825 and 1826 and to a certain extend influenced Valente's later design, particularly in terms of the two low side elements,

South facade looking toward the sea.

and perhaps also the main body of the building.

This aristocratic dwelling is quite different from contemporary neoclassical structures in Naples, both in the layout, which responds to English customs, and in the grandeur of the solutions, such as the imposing colonnaded portico, which seems to recall ancient Pompeiian villas. Certain incongruities, such as the facade with Ionic pilasters on a neo-Doric portico, can be ascribed to disagreements between the English nobleman and the architect, which date back to 1830. Pietro Valente had to redraft some twenty-two versions of the villa, with the "extremely fickle owner changing his ideas from day to day," according to the architect's resume, filed with the Ministry of Education. Precisely because of these disputes, Acton turned to Guglielmo Bechi, a Tuscan, for the interior decoration.

Doric colonnade overlooking the garden, toward the sea.

One of the facades of the villa.

following pages, left
Circular balustrade on the second floor, looking toward the entrance atrium.

following pages, right
Circular opening to the entrance atrium.

Bechi is also responsible for the design of the garden, which is one of the few remaining in the area. Despite alterations, the park still preserves the original English-style layout designed by Bechi. A network of winding avenues amid rare trees of unusual beauty, such as the *Araucaria* ("monkey puzzle," or Australian pine), and tall oaks, magnolias, camellias, and palms.

The numerous stylistic incongruities have always been viewed critically by proponents of orthodox neoclassicism. The south elevation is Palladian in influence, the north, like the interiors, has Pompeiian references, and the stepped-back facade overlooking the Riviera di Chiaia has a juxtaposition of a Doric colonnade over a colossal Ionic order.

Upon the death of the English baronet, in 1841, the residence was purchased, along with much of the gardens, by the Frankfurt banker Karl Rothschild. To adapt the residence to this noble family's needs, the baron first brought in an architect from Paris to embellish the interior decorations. Dissatisfied the results, he requested the collaboration of architect Gaetano Genovese. He also had a building erected at the north end of the park; it had three floors of offices and became known as the Palazzina Rothschild.

The German family's fortunes in Italy were tied to the Bourbon dynasty, and in 1867, after the Bourbons had left Naples, the villa was sold to Prince Diego Aragona Pignatelli Cortes, duke of Monteleone. In 1886 his nephew married Rosa Fici of the dukes of Amalfi, and under this new ownership the villa became the site of one of the most frequented salons in the city.

The interior decorations and furnishings were completely renovated, and great care was given to the organization of the garden. The refined taste of Princess Rosina and her husband helped to transform this patrician dwelling into one of the most aristocratic meeting places in Italy, and indeed in all Europe. Over a span of sixty years, this noblewoman gathered a precious collection of porcelain and furnishings, an extensive library, and an important collection of approximately four thousand long-playing records of classical music and opera, all of which were later donated to the Italian state, in 1955, after her death.

After restoration work, the villa was opened to the pubic in 1960 and named the Museo Diego Aragona

The "red room."

following page
Ground-floor veranda, overlooking the garden toward the sea, through the double Doric colonnade, with neoclassical sculptures.

Pignatelli Cortes.

Visitors enter around the back of the building, through an elegant cantilevered roof and atrium, which, in the past, was used as a carriage entrance. The ground floor of the museum has preserved its princely character. The ballroom, now used for conferences and concerts, is furnished with precious mirrors and doors frescoed with musician cherubs, created between 1870 and 1880 by Vincenzo Paliotti, a painter from Rome. Many of the other rooms are decorated in opulent and eclectic taste and named for their predominant color. The "red room," probably designed by architect Gaetano Genovese, has a central ceiling painting that depicts the allegory of Architecture, and it includes the plan of the villa. But it is the dining room that best conveys the sense of an inhabited noble residence. The table is set with Limoges plates, silver cutlery, and English glassware bearing the coat of arms of the Pignatelli family. The *piano nobile* also has an extremely charming neoclassical veranda, formerly a winter garden, now adapted for exhibitions and concerts.

The second-floor spaces of the museum have been completely transformed. Some have been adapted for museum offices, others are used for changing exhibitions. Finally, there are small revival-style buildings within the park. These were created at the end of the nineteenth century and include a neo-Gothic turret, a Swiss chalet, and a conservatory. A building that was formerly set aside for household administration has become the Museo delle Carrozze, with a collection of nineteenth-century carriages and harnesses, donated in 1960 by Marchese Mario D'Alessandro di Civitanova.

Library, with Japanese vases.

Palazzo Ruffo della Scaletta

South facade looking toward the sea, overlooking the Riviera di Chiaia.

The view toward the rear garden, through the entrance porch colonnade on the ground floor.

The Palazzo Ruffo della Scaletta stands at number 202 Riviera di Chiaia. The preexisting building, renovated in the nineteenth century, belonged to the prince of Bisignano, Don Tiberio Carafa, Cavaliere del Toson d'Oro and Grandee of Spain. According to Carlo Celano, he "raised many lions at home. ... One of these ... was so tame it slept in the same room as the Prince and went with him in his boat and carriage, and could eat no food save that given him by the Prince's own hands. It was a delight for the boys of Chiaia, for when the Prince went down to roam the beaches, they would wrestle and tumble with it, just as if it were another boy. ..." The Carafa di Belvedere property, as Arnaldo Venditti has noted, was one of the largest in the area. Between 1832 and 1833 the residence was completely rebuilt by Guglielmo Bechi, who, according to Luigi Catalani, "embellished the courtyard, built about twenty rooms on the north side, and a large hall, 88 by 44 spans, adorned with very harmonious stuccowork, gilding and paintings." Bechi created the staircase on an octagonal plan. It led from a space divided into three parts by two rows of Corinthian columns that, again according to Arnaldo Venditti, "echoed Sangallo's scheme for the atrium of the Palazzo Farnese in Rome, which can be seen as the spatial projection of a serlian triforium, namely the option, in an elongated space, to have a central area covered with a barrel vault and two side areas covered with a flat ceiling."

C. N. Sasso has observed that "there is a beautiful peristyle of Corinthian columns, mentioned previously, and rather delicately executed, which run along the entire diameter of the large octagon. At first glance it seems that it goes all the way to the garden. But at the end, you realize that the entire colonnade to the right and left takes an unusual turn and leads to the splendid staircase of white marble and bright white stuccowork. ... This composition, while not ugly, is at very least extremely eccentric. In this regard, it is worth remembering that the staircase for the Palazzo Serra, on the Pizzofalcone

road, made famous by Milizia, had a similar configuration and was designed by Ferdinando Sanfelice, who was well known for this sort of imaginative element. It leads to a single apartment, where there was no need for a peristyle."

The atrium, covered with a white barrel vault, and the courtyard, with an internal perspective regularly punctuated in the lower portion by pilasters and openings, lead to the staircase. Beyond, a garden is visible, which escaped being swallowed up by later construction. An iron and glass clerestory opens up at the center of the hip roof of the staircase space. The dome is embellished with Pompeiian motifs, in a style popular at the time.

While there is some lack of clarity about the solution as a whole, seen in the connections of the various staircase elements and terraces, overall there is an original interpretation of space, in keeping with the taste of that era and the tradition of spectacular staircases in Naples.

Francesco Saverio Ferrari, colonel of the Bourbon engineers, renovated the

preceding page
Monumental staircase.

Monumental staircase decorated with statues and bas-reliefs.

exterior. The building then underwent considerable transformations, which altered its original configuration.

The Goethe Institute is located on the second floor. According to Sasso, Guglielmo Bechi "planned the entrance for this second splendid apartment in ebony and white alabaster; the first vestibule has a circular shape with a bowl-shaped vault; and the entire space has gleaming stuccowork in various colors. For the cornice he made a concave molding the color of porphyry, within which one could see a host of white cherubs pursuing a lion with a whip. Adjacent, there was a room with a forest motif and painted shepherds, then another Pompeii-inspired room, then finally the grand ballroom. ... Gilding, plaster, stuccowork, vivid colors, carvings of every sort, and rich paintings in Pompeian style produced a very pleasant and gay decorative scheme."

preceding pages, left
Octagonal dome of the monumental staircase.

preceding pages, right
Detail of the stuccowork decorations.

Detail of frescoed decorations.

The Corner Palace of the Galleria Umberto I

The structure between Via Santa Brigida and Via Municipio (later called Via Verdi) was the last significant element in the building scheme for the Galleria Umberto I. Work for the new complex began in 1887, after the presentation of five different proposals. The approved scheme, an alteration by engineer Emmanuele Rocco of a more theatrical version by Antonio Curri, an architect from Puglia, left the Palazzo Capone intact at the corner of Via Santa Brigida and Via Municipio. It was not until 1890, the year the Galleria was officially opened, on the occasion of Labor Day, that this area was addressed from a design perspective. A theater was planned for the courtyard of the new palace, a revision of the arrangement between the city and the Esquilino Company, which was entrusted with building the entire complex. This change followed a dispute that arose regarding the illegal construction of a top floor by the contractors. The revised plan called for the construction of a performance space, with the goal of continuing the tradition of the Teatro San Carlino. From what can be gleaned from the project, Roman architect Ernesto di Mauro, who was also the site superintendent, designed the theater according to a plan defined by the shape of the new building's courtyard. The perimeter was far enough away from the walls of the building to allow a comfortable passageway. In drawings, the horseshoe-shaped auditorium was turned inward, toward the stage, which was preceded by the orchestra pit. Running all the way round, four tiers of box seats provide an unusual solution for joining the two opposite sides. The urban-planning role of connecting this space with other preexisting and

Galleria Umberto I: east wing.

following pages, left
Corner palazzo of the Galleria Umberto I: facade outside the Galleria.

following pages, right
Corner palazzo of the Galleria Umberto I: entrance arch leading from the central octagon of the Galleria.

CENTRO
luxor radio

functional spaces coexists with the palazzo's self-sufficiency and its appropriation of certain functions of the surrounding areas.

Once the Palazzo Capone was demolished, the need to renovate the entire building block naturally involved considerable financial interests. After inquiries were made about obtaining necessary funding, numerous projects were proposed. Between July 1893 and January 1894 proposals were put forth by: Stampa de Angelis e Co.; Francesco Carrelli, the engineer who had previously overseen work on the nearby church of Santa Brigida and who was backed by Banca d'Italia; Emmanuele Rocco, an engineer who proposed a lump-sum contract; two interrelated proposals by Gaetano Rossi Romano, an attorney; a proposal by Opere Pubbliche del Mezzogiorno d'Italia, which had presented a request two years before; and finally a project by engineer Michele Franchini. All these proposals called for the maximum use of the available space, with an exterior imbued with dignity by the organization of the facades in accordance with the usual modulations of neo-Renaissance taste. The plan by Esquilino, which was approved by the municipal technical council in 1894, takes full advantage of the space. Its written description states that "since the cutting off of the corner (of the entrance from the

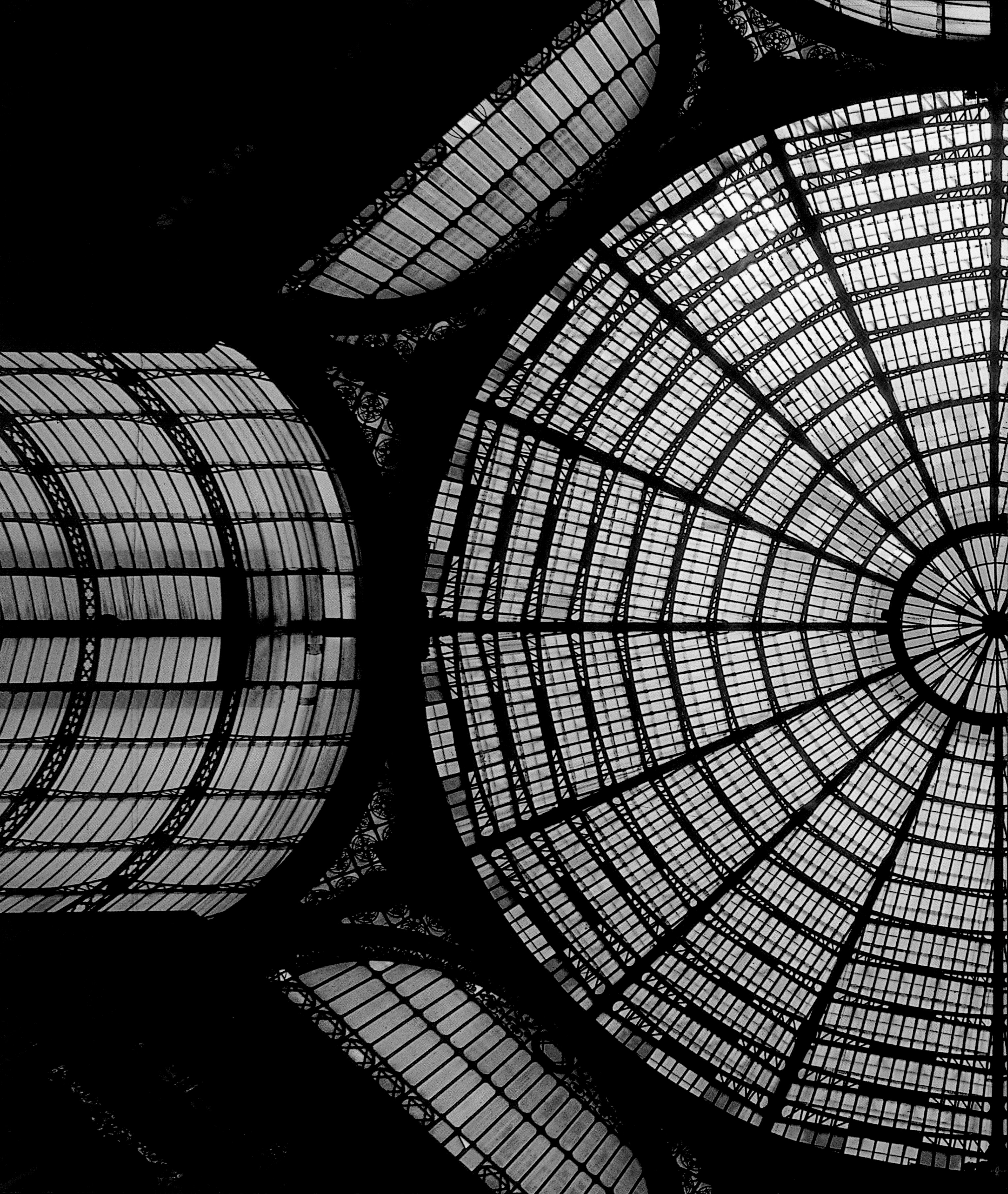

street) and the consequent decoration would entail ruining valuable area and greater expense, a decision was made to eliminate this cut at the corner of the building and consequently the entrance hall to the Galleria. With the elimination of these elements, an additional income of approximately 10,000 lire could be obtained, also doing away with the concomitant burden to create a passageway."

The entrance to the building—in fact, later created with the cutting off of the corner—was studied in depth. The different proposals alternated between attempts to guarantee maximum dignity and efforts to keep the design compatible with the characteristics of the Galleria. But beyond the specific qualities that distinguish the entrance of the new building, it is interesting to note how the solution of an architectural problem was achieved through criteria that were extrinsic and extraneous to a freely inventive process. Criteria of general dignity and a desire for uniformity with contiguous parts almost automatically dictated conformity with a combination of aesthetic motifs that seem to be put together like interchangeable pieces of a toy. In the various solutions, the entrance was frequently disassembled and put back together according to competing proposals by various professionals, until an "objectively" acceptable design was reached. This design process was basically influenced by the overall appearance of the entire Galleria. The question of the corner cut is a mere detail in terms of the entire project, while the modifications to the design and aesthetic decisions regarding that element are in some way indicative of the criteria that governed the taste of the time.

In its totality the palazzo

preceding page
Galleria Umberto I: windowed dome with sixteen segments.

Atrium leading from the Galleria.

"Serlian" window motif looking into the Galleria.

1890

reproposes "bourgeois" building canons, which aim to "extract the greatest possible number of habitable spaces and consequently the greatest possible income, while respecting, in terms of the exterior, the building's required architecture." This quote appeared in the report that accompanied one of the proposals.

The building had six stories, including the "attic story," which was crowned above by a prominent cornice, punctuated by strongly projecting corbels. A stringcourse band extends to the bottom portion of the building—which included spaces for stores, surmounted by an intermediary level, lower in height and, on the third level, an ample rectangular space. This stringcourse unifies the balustrades of the balconies to the small columns. The two principal residential floors and the narrow attic level lie above. Within the courtyard, one can still see vestiges of the metal cantilevered roof that ran along the perimeter, supported by extremely slender cast-iron columns, which in turn rest upon a stone balustrade. This latter element was covered by a raised walkway, which allowed light into the spaces below. In a letter from Emmanuele Rocco to Esquilino, dated 14 April 1896, the engineer writes of his decision to construct the balustrade out of masonry mortar. The walkway was made with Hennebique (reinforced concrete) floors. Certain elements of the design undoubtedly had to be simplified, such as the metal corbels supporting the roof, originally meant to be independent flanges, which instead became integral elements. Today, a metal lip indicated in the drawings is missing, and the two curving staircases that led to the raised walkway level have been destroyed. But the building still has a welcoming aspect, due to the enveloping configuration of the open, lowered space, which gives the tall walls a sort of "scale" in proportion to the planar dimensions of the courtyard. Construction was completed between 1898 and 1899.

"Serlian" portico between the landing and the interior staircase.

Grand Eden Hotel

Between the final years of the nineteenth century and the early years of the new century, the Grand Eden Hotel was built, above the Piazza Amedeo, which would become the heart of the new Chiaia residential quarter. The piazza was one of the few elements built from the plan for the quarter that was devised in 1859 by architects Alvino, Cangiano, Gauvadan, Francesconi, and Saponieri. The urbanization of the district concluded toward the end of the nineteenth century, with the creation of the Via Vittoria Colonna, Via dei Mille, Via Filangieri, and finally the Via del Parco Margherita.

Wealthy foreigners frequently stayed in Naples for long periods, drawn by the beauty of the climate and the remarkable sites. This led Giulio Huraut, husband of Maria Genevois—who belonged to an important French family of entrepreneurs with whom he had already been associated—to construct a new hotel. He entrusted the project to Angelo Trevisan, an engineer from the Veneto.

The construction of the grand structure was meant to complete the new piazza, which already had the Palazzo Balzorano and the Villino Colonna Pignatelli on its west side. The latter was built in 1878, and its garden with curving avenues and flower beds was completed about two years later. The principal characteristic of the new urban space—in an area of the city that was, at that time, in the process of being built up—was a sort of tree-filled piazza. Buildings facing the piazza were all stepped back from the street and concealed by lawns and tall plants. The Grand Eden Hotel conformed to this standard until 1925, when the gardens of the Villino Colonna Pignatelli were occupied by a new massive building by Giulio Ulisse Arata. At that time the small subway station building was also added.

Huraut's grand hotel, completed in 1901, represents a new element in the urban

Pavilion of the former winter garden.

Garden, looking toward Piazza Amedeo, with the sea behind.

Central tower.

and architectural panorama of the city. In terms of its setting, it resolves the backdrop above the piazza with a building of unusual scale but a theatrical participant in the natural context in which it was placed. Architecturally, it anticipated the eclectic style that would develop in Naples some years later, marked by a total indifference to consistency of elements, assembled with the sole intention of shaping a harmonious and original whole, organically faithful to naturalistic elements and to the nature of the site.

The original project was the result of a careful study of formal and architectural motifs then in vogue, with particular reference to traditions of the Veneto and French culture. It was never completed because of economic difficulties, which prevented some elements from being built as planned. Sited on steep terrain, Huraut's property extended as far as the hillside of the Corso Vittorio Emanuele, which lay above. The building was located behind

preceding pages, left
Detail of the spiral base of the half columns in the pavilion of the former winter garden.

preceding pages, right
One of the access ramps winding around the pavilion of the former winter garden.

A window of the former winter garden, originally with glassed-in walls.

Domical vault of the entrance vestibule.

Detail of the pictorial decorations of the edge of the domical vault of the entrance vestibule.

the hill, thus leaving open the sloping green area in front. This area was organized as a park and filled with exotic plants and fruit trees, with benches and cast-iron lanterns set among flower beds and winding paths, the layout of which had been studied in order to compensate for the steepness of the land.

The main entrance, which consists of a double, pincer-shaped flight of steps, was approached by a straight avenue along the Balzorani property. The elliptical ramps of the staircase encircle part of the building that was originally glassed in and used as a winter garden, but was later filled in with masonry. The steps are Carrara marble, each a single piece, and the handrail, of which only the left side remains, is skillfully worked tufa and follows the sinuous curve of the ramp.

The wonderful iron and glass cantilevered roof extended out far enough that it constituted an exterior structure, but it collapsed in 1970 and no physical evidence or documentation remains.

The entrance atrium, which branches off into the principal reception spaces, is covered by a vault frescoed with Art Nouveau designs, with vine shoots and floral motifs. A profile of a woman is depicted against a trellis. In front of the entrance, the winter garden—with three slightly curved sides and entirely glassed in, with curved fixtures with fanciful designs—was a covered space with a slightly domed vault decorated with the usual ornamental motifs. It was like a transparent bubble, set among the plants of the park.

After the atrium, another space, covered with a flat ceiling decorated with floral motifs, leads into the reception rooms (part of which once was the hotel offices, then the apartment of Maria Genevois). A three-flight staircase and an elevator lie beyond.

On the second floor, one proceeds from the landing to an opulent staircase, which in turn leads to the dining room, with shiny stucco columns and, to the right, the kitchen spaces. The staircase was later modified.

On the east facade, a secondary entrance, through an elegant portal, made it possible to avoid traveling the entire Via di Parco Margherita as far as the piazza. It was never finished according to its original plan and was subjected to later modifications. Nonetheless, the Grand Eden Hotel remains an emblematic example of the eclectic taste and the culture that predominated in Naples during the years spanning the passage from the nineteenth to the twentieth century.

Castello Aselmeyer and Villa Ebe

Castello Aselmeyer is a particularly interesting example of the eclectic style in Naples because of its attention to the use of natural materials.

The designer, engineer Lamont Young, was born in Naples on 12 March 1851 to an English father and Indian mother. He was educated in Switzerland and England, and the Neapolitan environment had little impact on his upbringing, although he was exposed to the entrepreneurial spirit and the day-to-day problems that affected many of his fellow citizens.

In 1899 he purchased from the municipality some land left over from property expropriated for work on the Corso Vittorio Emanuele where it runs into the Parco Grifeo. His intention was to create a grand hotel, with the entrance on the new road, but at first he built only a portico with a concierge's house. Between 1902 and 1904 he purchased other properties from Banca d'Italia and from Baron Corsi, on which he created gardens.

Construction developed in two distinct areas. A lower structure, between two small towers, was finished in rough rustication in Vesuvian stone. This was linked to an upper

Development of the facades overlooking Corso Vittorio Emanuele.

West tower.

following page
Terraces looking toward the sea.

structure by an elevator and by a winding staircase, cut into the rock and interrupted by small terraces. The tufa was reshaped to accommodate the construction, so that it is possible to say that this work is the result of an inseparable marriage between an architecture that, in form and materials, tends toward nature, and a natural setting that has been adapted to the built project.

The irregular rocky surface contains many holes and cavities. Young utilized these, tunneling to the back of the building and linking them with vents or vertical air chambers, which served to insulate the palazzo from the hillside and to ventilate the back part of the building. This was a common construction practice in Indian architecture, which apparently was familiar to the designer through his maternal ancestry. The project as a whole draws one of its principal characteristics from the rhythm created by the projections and recesses of the crenellated volumes, as well as from the contrast of the rusticated surface against the trim of the windows, the bow windows, and the loggia with its small spiral columns. Even with this great variety of elements, there is a unifying aesthetic.

The entrance hall is very elegant, characterized by a vaulted ceiling that uninterruptedly continues the elements on the facade, emphasized by the slender, white ribbing in relief, which brings together the entire space. The other interior spaces, inspired by similar aesthetic criteria, are typical of neo-Gothic revival taste, refined by a sinuousness of line that is specific to Young's exotic style.

In 1904 Young sold the property to Carlo Aselmeyer, a banker, and then moved to the island of Gajola, beneath the Posillipo promontory. Subsequently the property, originally meant to accommodate only two large apartments, was subdivided into numerous residences. Two large volumes added to the lower building negatively altered the overall image, and the vertical vents in the rear—an integral part of the building's logic and its merging with the natural setting—were closed off to utilize the rear spaces for service structures.

Many permanent furnish-ings and wooden fixtures remain in the interior spaces, such as pointed-arch door-ways, door and window frames, and wooden ceilings. About twenty years after designing the Castello Aselmeyer, Lamont Young built the Villa Ebe, along the Via Chiatamone ramps. This project once again is characterized by a refined rustic style that draws on local architectural styles.

The Villa Ebe was preceded by a futuristic, utopian project for a large hotel with an iron and glass dome, in neo-Indian style,

Terraces overlooking the sea.

Interior staircase of Lamont Young's residence.

with many terraces, pavil ions, and minarets, but this was never approved by the municipality.

Lamont Young then returned to the idea of a sort of second "Castle Lamont," on terrain he had purchased between 1914 and 1915 on state land along the Via Santa Lucia and the Chiatamone ramps. Here too, he created a building on two different levels, in two distinct elements, one intended for the Astarita family and the other for his own family's residence—named Villa Ebe after his wife.

Only the Villa Ebe survived the bombardments of World War II. It has a square tower with octagonal buttresses in Vesuvian stone, with building elements in tufa, embellished with arched windows, bow windows, all in the eclectic and orientalizing style typical of Lamont Young, for whom time apparently had stopped with the creation of the Castello Aselmeyer.

Here, too, as in the structure on the Corso Vittorio Emanuele, the wooden ceilings, doors, and staircase have remained for the most part intact and still provide us with an illustration of this eclectic style of residential interiors.

preceding page
Detail of the floor tiles on a terrace of Castello Aselmeyer.

Access ramps along the slopes of Monte Echia, overlooking the sea.

The central building element.

The authors and publisher would like to thank the following people and organizations for their invaluable help:

Municipality of Naples—ufficio Cultura, Ente Ville Vesuviane, Goethe Institut, Istituto Italiano per gli Studi Storici, Istituto Italiano per gli Studi Filosofici, Istituto Pimentel Fonseca, Istituto Universitario Navale, Istiuto Universitario Orientale, Museo Civico Filangieri, Museo della Ceramica duca di Martina, Museo Nazionale di Capodimonte, Museo principe Diego Aragona Pignatelli Cortes, Archives Offices, Soprintendenza BBAAAA, Naples; Soprintendenze BBAASS, Naples and region; Court of Naples—Bankruptcy Division; University of Naples Federico II—School of Agriculture; University of Naples Federico II—School of Architecture

Mario Agrimi, Alfonso Artiaco, Sergio Attanasio, Nadia Barrella, Umberto Basile, Pasquale Belfiore, Antonio Brandi, Raffaele Calace, Francesco Calandro, Fernanda Capobianco, Aristide Caputo, Francesco Cassano, Felice Casucci, Giovanni Battista Ciotti, Marina Colonna, Maria Luisa Colonna Spalletti, Diodato Colonnesi, Alda Croce, Silvia Croce, Carla d'Allocco, Francesco d'Aquino di Caramanico, Nicoletta D'Arbitrio, Effrem de Angelis, Maria Luisa de Divitiis, Ezio De Felice, Ennio De Rosa, Augusto de Luzenberger, Maria Edvige de Palama Balice, Luigi Desiato, Gennaro Di Natale, Rosaria Famularo, Gennaro Ferrara, Angerio Filangieri, Salvatore Fiore, Katia Fiorentino, Maria Antonietta Gambriglia, Antonio Gargano, Francesco Garzilli, Gianantonio Garzilli, Giovanni Genova, Paola Giusti, Marta Herling, Carlo Longobardi, Giuseppe Mannajuolo, Manuia S.p.A., Marisa Margiotta, Francesco Marigliano Caracciolo, Gerardo Marotta, Arturo Martorelli, Luisa Martorelli, Stefano Mazzoleni, Morano Editore S.p.A., Giuseppe Morra, Riccardo Motti, Carmine Noviello, Denise Pagano, Dr. Pagliuca [Office for Vesuvian Villas 081 412626/405393], Massimo Pisani, Annalisa Porzio, Giulio Raimondi, Francesco Ricciardi, Massimo Ricciardi, Lilia Rocco, Paolo Romanello, Hellen Rotolo, Filomena Sardella, Eirene Sbriziolo, Fulvio Simeoni, Nicola Spinosa, Maria Tagliatela, Maurizio Tarantino, Angela Tecce, Mr. Trematerre (forest-land for the Royal Palace at Capodimonte, see architect Carughi), Paolo Vezza, Sergio Villari, Giuseppe Zampino, Luigi Ziviello

Selected bibliography

ACTON F., *Il museo civico Gaetano Filangieri di Napoli,* Naples 1986.
ALISIO G., *Napoli nel Seicento. Le vedute di Francesco Cassiano de Silva,* Naples 1974.
———. *Siti reali dei Borboni,* Rome 1976.
———. *Lamont Young. Utopia e realtà nell'urbanistica napoletana dell'Ottocento,* Rome 1978.
———. *Urbanistica Napoletana del Settecento,* Bari 1979.
———. *Napoli e il risanamento. Recupero di una struttura,* Naples 1980.
———., ed. *Gino Doria—I palazzi di Napoli,* Naples 1992.
All'ombra del Vesuvio. Napoli nella veduta europea dal Quattrocento all'Ottocento, exhibition catalog, Naples 1990.
ASSUNTO R., *La città di Anfione e la cittàdi Prometeo,* Milan 1983.
ATTANASIO S., *La Villa Carafa di Belvedere al Vomero,* Naples 1985.

BELFIORE P., *Costruzione e decostruzione,* in Mazzoleni D. and Belfiore P., *Metapolis. Strutture e storia di una grande città,* Rome 1983.
BELMONTE T. *The Broken Fountain,* New York 1979.
BILE U. and LUCA DAZIO M., *Capodimonte da Reggia a museo,* Pozzuoli 1995.

CANTONE G., *Il palazzo Maddaloni allo Spirito Santo,* Naples 1979.
———., *Napoli Barocca,* Bari 1993.
CAPACCIO G.C., *Il Forastiero,* Naples 1634.
CARUGI U., *La Galleria Umberto I. Architettura del ferro a Napoli,* Naples 1992.
———., ed. *Segno, Metodo, Progetto. Itinerari dell'immagine urbana tra memoria e intervento,* Naples 1990.
———., ed. *Spaccanapoli. Centro Storico,* Naples 1992.
CATALANI L. *I palazzi di Napoli,* Naples 1845.
CAUSA PICONE M. and Porzio A., *Il Palazzo Reale di Napoli,* Naples 1986.
CECI G., "Il palazzo Penna," in *Napoli Nobilissima,* Naples January 1894.
CELANO C., *Notizie del bello dell'antico e del curioso della cittàdi Napoli per i signori forestieri date dal canonico C.C. Celano, divise in dieci giornate in ognuna delle quali si assegnano le strade per dove bassi a camminare dedicate alla Santitàdi N.S. Papa Innocenzo XII,* 10 vols., Naples, 1692-97.
CELANO C. and CHIARINI G.B., *Notizie del bello dell'antico e del curioso della citta di Napoli,* 5 vols., 1856-1860, 1870, 1970, 1974, 1976, 1978.
CHAMBERS I., *Paesaggi migratori,* Naples 1998.
Le città di fondazione, Venice 1978.
Civilitàdel Seicento a Napoli, Naples 1984.
Civilità del Settecento a Napoli, Naples 1979.
Le collezioni del museo di Capodimonte, Naples 1982.
COLONNESI D., *Palazzo Marigliano,* Naples 1998.
CROCE B., "Il palazzo Bisignano poi Filomarino," in *Storia del regno di Napoli,* Bari 1958.

D'AMBRA R., *Napoli antica,* Naples 1889.
D'ARBITRIO N. and ZIVIELLO L., *Dal Grand Eden Hotel di piazza Amedeo alla fabbrica Cirio di Vigliena,* Naples 1992.
DE DIVITIIS PAGANO G., *Il napoletano palazzo di Venezia,* Naples 1980.
DE MARINIS L., *Cenni storici sulla Villa "Belvedere" al Vomero (Naples),* Naples 1945.
DE SETA C., *Storia della citta di Napoli dalle origini al Settecento,* Bari 1973.
———., *Architettura ambiente e società a Napoli nel '700,* Turin 1981.
———., *Le città nella Storia d'Italia. Naples,* Bari 1988.
DI MAURO L., "L'eruzione del Vesuvio nel 1631," in *Civiltà del Seicento a Napoli,* Naples 1984.
DI RESTA I., "Il palazzo napoletano nel XVI secolo," in Valtieri, S., ed., *Il palazzo dal Rinascimento ad oggi,* s.d.
DORIA G., *Carnet del turista,* Naples 1958-1959.
DORIA G.,BOLOGNA F., and PANNAIN G., *Settecento napoletano,* Turin 1962.
DORIA G. and CAUSA R., *I tesori—La Reggia di Capodimonte,* Florence 1966.

Facciate delli palazzi piùcospicui della città di Napoli, Naples 1718.
FIENGO G., *Gioffredo e Vanvitelli nei palazzi dei Casacalenda,* Naples 1976.
FILANGIERI R., *I Banchi di Napoli dalle origini alla costituzione del Banco delle due Sicilie (1539-1808),* Naples 1940.

GALANTI G.M., *Guida storico-monumentale della cittàdi Napoli e contorni,* edited by L. Galanti, Naples 1829.
GARZYA C., *Interni neoclassici a Napoli,* Naples 1978.
GIANNETTI A.and MUZII R., *Antonio Niccolini architetto e scenografo alla corte di Napoli (1807-1850),* Naples 1998.
GIORDANO P., *Ferdinando Fuga a Napoli. L'Albergo dei Poveri, il Cimitero delle 366 fosse, i Granili,* Lecce 1997.

GIUSTI P., ed. *Il museo Duca di Martina di Napoli*, Naples 1994.
GUELFO M., ed. *Gli intestini di Napoli*, Naples 1982.

LABROT G., *Palazzi napoletani. Storie di nobili e cortigiani 1520-1750*, Naples 1993.
LATTUADA R., *Il Barocco a Napoli e in Campania*, Naples 1988.
LENZA C., *Monumento e Tip nell'architettura neoclassica. L'opera di Pietro Valente nella cultura napoletana dell'800*, Naples 1996.

MACCI F., *Museo Cappella Sansevero*, Casoria 1998.
MANGONE F., *Giulio Ulisse Arata. Opera completa*, Naples 1993.
———., *Pietro Valente*, Naples 1996.
MANGONE F.and SCALVINI, M. L., *Arata a Napoli tra liberty e neoclassicismo*, Naples 1990.
MARRONE R., ed. *Le strade di Napoli*, vol II, year II, no. 22, Naples 1992.
MAZZOLENI D., *Tra Castel dell'Ovo e Sant'Elmo. Napoli: il percorso delle origini*, Naples 1995.
———., "Metastrutture., Napoli: la differenza e la catastrofe," in *La Nuovea Citta*, 5 December 1984.
———., "Napoli e ilrituale di fondazione," in Paba, G., ed. *La citta e il limite*, Florence 1990.
———., "The City and the Imaginary," in E. Carter, J. Donald, and J. Squires, ed. *Space & Place. Theories of Identity and Location*. London 1993.
———., "Il vuoto e le cose," in *Le lingue di Napoli*, Naples 1994.
———., ed. *La città e l'immaginario*, Rome 1985.
———., ed. *Nature Architecture Diversity/Natura Architettura Diversita*, Naples 1998.
MAZZOLENI D.; Belfiore, Pasquale, *Metapolis. Strutture e storia di una grande citta*, Rome 1983.
MAZZOLENI S. and MAZZOLENI D., *L'Orto Botanico di Portici*, Naples 1990.
MUROLO M. G., *Una villa napoletana del Seicento. Villa Belvedere*, Rome 1967.

Napoli antica, Naples 1985.
Napoli Città d'Arte, Naples 1986.
NIOLA M., *Sui palchi delle stelle*, Rome 1995.

ORTESE A.M., *Il mare non bagna Napoli*, Milan 1975.

Palazzo Corigliano tra Archaeologia e Storia, Naples 1985.
Il Palazzo Reale di Napoli, Naples 1986.
Il Palazzo Reale di Napoli, Naples 1994.
Il Palazzo Reale di Napoli, Naples 1995.
PANE R., *Architettura del Rinascimento in Napoli*, Naples 1937.
———., *Architettura dell'età barocca in Napoli*, Naples 1949.
———., *Napoli imprevista*, Naples 1949.
———., *Ferdinando Fuga*, Naples 1956.
———., *Il Rinascimento nell'Italia meridionale*, Milan 1975.
———., "Architettura e urbanistica del Rinascimento," in *Storia di Napoli*, 4 vols., I, Cava dei Tirreni 1974.
———., ed., *Seicento napoletano. Arte, costume, ambiente*, Milan 1984.
PANE R., ALISIO, G., DI MONDA P., SANTORO L., and VENDITTI A., *Ville vesuviane del Settecento*, Naples 1959.
PANE G.and VALERIO V., ed. *La citta di Napoli tra vedutismo e cartografia. Piante e vedute dal XV al XIX secolo*, Naples 1987.
PESSOLANO M. R. , *Il palazzo d'Angri. Un'opera napoletana tra Tardobarocco e Neoclassicismo*, Naples 1980.
La pittura in Italia. Il Settecento, ed. G. Briganti, Milan 1989-1990.

RAMONDINO F.and MÜLLER A. F., *Dadapolis. Caleidoscopio napoletano*, Turin 1889.
La reggia di Portici, Naples 1998.
RIZZO V., *Un architetto di gusto palladiano a Napoli: Trojano Spinelli duca di Laurino. Il rifacimento settecentesco del suo palazzo*, Aversa 1988.
RUOTOLO R., *Mercanti-collezionisti fiamminghi a Napoli. Gaspare Roomer e i Vandeneynden*, Massa Lubrense 1982.
RYKWERT J., *The Idea of a Town*, 1976.

SASSO C.N., *Storia dei monumenti di Napoli e degli architetti che li edificavano*, Naples 1856-1858.
SAVARESE L., *Il centro antico di Napoli. Analisi delle trasformazioni urbane*, Naples 1991.
SAVARESE S., *Palazzo Cellammare. La stratificazione di una dimora aristocratica (1540-1730)*, Naples 1996.
Storia di Napoli, Cava dei Tirreni 1974.
Storia e Civilta dellà Campania. Il Settecento, Naples 1994.
STRAZZULLO F., *Edilizia e urbanistica a Napoli dal '500 al '700*, Naples 1968.
———., ed. *Palazzo di Capua*, Naples 1995.

TECCE A., ed. *Il museo Pignatelli di Napoli*, Naples 1994.
Il Trionfo della miseria, Milan 1995.

VENDITTI A., *Architettura neoclassica a Napoli*, Naples 1961.
———., "Urbanistica e Architettura nella Napoli angioina," in *Storia di Napoli*, vol. III, Naples 1972.
———., "Presenze e influenze catalane nell'architettura napoletana del Regno d'Aragona(1442-1503)," in *Napoli Nobilisima*, vol. XIII, no. I, Naples 1974.
Villa Vesuviane, Milan 1980.
Ville Vesuviane. Progetto per un patrimonio settecentesco di urbanistica e architettura, Naples 1988.
La voce della Campania, Salerno 1983.

Addresses of palaces

Albergo dei Poveri
Piazza Carlo III
Closed to the public.

Sansevero Chapel
Via De Sanctis 19
Open to the public:
weekdays 10 a.m.-5 p.m.;
weekends 10 a.m.–1:30 p.m.;
closed Tuesday.

Palazzo Carafa di Maddaloni
Via San Biagio dei Librai 121
The courtyard is open to the public on weekdays.

Palazzo Casacalenda
Piazza San Domenico Maggiore 17
The courtyard is open to the public on weekdays.

Palazzo Casamassima
Via Banchi Nuovi 8
The courtyard is open to the public on weekdays.

Castello Aselmeyer
Corso Vittorio Emanuele 166
Closed to the public.

Palazzo Cellamare
Via Chiaia 149
Closed to the public.

Palazzo Corigliano
Piazza San Domenico Maggiore 12
Istituto Universitario Orientale
Open to the public on weekdays.

Palazzo Cuomo
Via Dumo 288
Museo Civico Filangieri
Open to the public:
weekdays 9:30 a.m. – 2p.m.,
3:30 p.m, -7 p.m.;
weekends 9:30 a.m. – 1:30 p.m.

Palazzo dello Spagnuolo
Via Vergini 19
The courtyard is open to the public on weekdays.

Palazzo Donn'Anna
Via Posillipo 9
Closed to the public.

Palazzo D'Angri
Piazza VII Settembre 28
The courtyard is open to the public on weekdays.

Palazzo Filomarino
via Benedetto Croce 12
Istituto Italiano per gli Studi Storici e Fondazione Croce
The library is open to the public on Tuesdays and Fridays from 9 a.m.-1 p.m.

Grand Eden Hotel
Piazza Amedeo 14
Closed to the public.

Palazzo Maddaloni
Via Maddaloni 6
The courtyard is open to the public on weekdays.

Palazzo Marigliano
Via San Biagio dei Librai 39
Soprintendenza Archivestica (Government Archive Office)
Open to the public:
Monday through Friday,
10 a.m. – 1 p.m.

Palazzo d'angolodella Galleria Umberto I
Corner of Via Santa Brigida and Via Verdi
The Galleria (covered arcade) is open to the public.

Palazzo Penne
Piazzetta Monticelli 11
The courtyard is open to the public on weekdays.

Palazzo Petrucci
Piazza San Domenico Maggiore 3
The courtyard is open to the public on weekdays.

Palazzo Reale
Piazza Plebiscito 11
Museo Nazionale di Palazzo Reale
Open to the public:
Monday through Friday,
9:30 a.m.– 9 p.m.,
Saturday 9:30 a.m. – midnight,
Sunday 9:30 a.m. – 8 p.m.,
closed Wednesday.

Palazzo Reale di Capodimonte
Via Capodimonte
Museo Nazionale di Capodimonte
Open to the public weekdays 10 a.m.- 7 p.m., Sunday 9 a.m. – 8 p.m., closed Monday.

Palazzo Reale di Portici
Portici (Naples)
School of Agriculture
Open to the public on weekdays.

Palazzo Ruffo della Scaletta
Riviera di Chiaia 202.
Open to the public:
Monday through Friday,
9 a.m. – 1 p.m.,
2 p.m. – 5 p.m.

Palazzo Sanfelice
Via Arena alla Sanità 2-6
The courtyard is open to the public on weekdays.

Palazzo Sansevero
Piazza San Domenico Maggiore 9
The courtyard is open to the public on weekdays.

Palazzo Serra di Cassano
Via Egiziaca a Pizzofalcone 67
Istituto italiano per gli studi filosofici (Italian Institute for Philosophical Studies)
Open to the public on weekdays, 9 a.m. – 8 p.m.

Palazzo Venezia
Via Benedetto Croce 19
The courtyard is open to the public on weekdays.

Villa Acton Pignatelli
Riviera di Chiaia 200
Museo principe Diego Aragona Pignatelli Cortes
Open to the public:
weekdays, 9 a.m. – 2 p.m.;
weekends (the garden only), 9 a.m. 1 p.m.

Villa Campolieto
Portici (Naples)
Ente ville vesuviane (Government office for Vesuvian Villas)
Open to the public Tuesday – Sunday, 10 a.m. – 1 p.m., closed Monday.

Villa Ebe
Rampe Lamont Young
Closed to the public.

Villa Floridiana
Via Cimarosa – Via Aniello Falcone
Museo nazionale duca di Martina
Open to the public Tuesday – Sunday, 9 a.m. – 2 p.m., closed Monday.

Index of names and places

The names of the palaces described in detail in this volume are in capital letters.

abate di Stigliano 84
Acton, Ferdinand 266, 272
Alfonso d'Aragona duca di Calabria 44, 55
Algeri 10
Alisio, Giancarlo 179, 196, 199
Alvino, Errico 298
Amalfi, Carlo 104
Amendola, Giovan Battista 139
ammiraglio di Castiglia 157
Andreuccio da Perugia 36
Angelini, Costanzo 206
Angelini, Tito 187
Angiò (family) 135
Aosta, Dukes of (family) 188
Aragona Pignatelli Cortes, Diego Duke of Monteleone 272
Arata, Giulio Ulisse 298
Asburgo (family) 119
Aselmeyer, Carlo 311
Astarita (family) 314
Astarita, Giuseppe 167, 240, 243
Atene 10
Atienza, Tommaso 167
Avellino, Prince of 131
Avena, Adolfo 158

Balducci, Goivanni 135
Baratta, Alessandro 17, 250
Barcellona 10
Barra 195
Barra, Didier 23
Batoni, Pompeo 244
Bechi, Guglielmo 272, 278, 286
Belfiore, Pasquale 29
Belliazzi, Reffaele 139
Benedetto XIV, Pope 112
Benincasa, Giovanni 132
Benjamin, Walter 10
Berlino, Charlottenburg 195
Bernardino, Nicola 63
Bianchi, Pietro 136
Bisignano (family) 59
Bisogni, Gennaro 201
Bonaparte, Giuseppe 187, 260
Bonaparte, Napoleone 59
Bonavia, Carlo 26
Bonito, Giuseppe 190, 201, 202, 244
Borgia, Duke 236
Borgia, Stefano Cardinal 190
Borrelli, Gian Giotto 120
Bottigilieri, Felice 76
Bottiglieri, Matteo 71
Bourbon (family) 119, 142, 176, 187, 192, 210, 219, 272
Bramante, Donato 71
Brancaccio (family) 52, 59, 60, 63
Breglia, Nicola 158
Bulifon, Antonio 20
Buonocore, Filippo 119, 120

Caggiano, Emanuele 139
Califano, Giuseppe 42
Cambi, Tommaso 78
Cammarano, Giuseppe 142, 148, 261
Canevari, Antonio 179, 195, 215
Cangiano, Luigi 298
Canova, Antonio 183
Capaccio, Guilio Cesare 15, 20
Capano (family) 41
Capano, Giovanni Gerolamo 41
Capasso, Bartolomeo 68
Capone 59
Capua 28
Caracciolo, Battistello 135, 146, 190
Caracciolo, Girolama 104
Caracciolo, Sergianni 150
Caracciolo, Tommaso, Prince of Colubrano 131
Carafa (family) 41, 266
Carafa della Spina, Adriana 104
Carafa di Belvedere (family) 278
Carafa di Maddaloni (family) 131
Carafa di Maddaloni, Diomede 127, 128
Carafa di Stigliano, Clarice 104
Carafa di Stigliano, Luigi 84
Carafa, Anna 150, 154, 157
Carafa, Diomede 41, 42
Carafa, Tiberio, Prince of Bisignano, Knight of Toson d'Oro and Grandee of Spain 278
Carafa, Giovanni, Duke of Noja 28, 226, 250
Carafa, Giuseppe 128
Caramanico, Prince of 195
Carasale, Angelo 179
Caravaggio (Michelangelo Merisi) 190
Cardarelli 195
Carelli, Leonardo 240
Caracci, Agostino 190
Caracci, Annibale 190
Carrelli, Francesco 294
Cascalenda (family) 244
Caserta 10
reggia 29, 37, 136, 183, 192, 196, 199, 201, 216, 229, 253
Castellmare di Stabia 46
Catalani, Luigi 67, 94, 97, 278
Catalani, Sigismondo 42
Catemario, Duke of 131
Cavallino, Bernardo 190
Ceci, Giuseppe 41
Celano, Carlo 42, 192, 278
Celebrano, Francesco 97, 101, 104, 109
Cestaro, Jacopo 230, 234
Charles Bourbon 76, 112, 135, 146, 176, 179, 180, 192, 199, 201, 215, 250
Charles of Anjou 44
Charles III 187
Charles III of Durazzo 52
Charles IV of Austria 112
Charles VI of Austria 101
Chaux 30
Cimarosa, Domenico 142
Cioffi, Rosanna 98, 112
Clay 149
Cobianchi, Giovanni 209
Codazzi, Viviano 148, 157
Colantonio190
Colonnessi, Diodato 76
Compagno, Scipione 23
Confalonieri 135
Confuorto 20
Coppola, Carlo 23
Corenzio, Belisario 135, 142
Corigliano (family) 116
Corigliano 122
Corigliano, Giacomo 116
Corniani, Gian Giacomo 52, 59
Corradini, Antonio 101, 104, 109
Corregio (Antonio Allegri) 190
Corsi, Baron 306
Cosentino, Donato 236
Cottrau, Alfredo 46
Croce, Benedetto 60, 64, 67
Cuomo (family) 44, 46
Cuomo, Angelo 44, 46
Cuomo, Giovanni 44
Cuomo, Leonardo 46
Curri, Antonio 288
d'Adamo, Carlo 76
d'Alessandro, Giovanni 240
D'Alessandro, Mario, Marquis of Civitanova 276
Danckerts, C. 17
da Nola, Giovanni 93, 94
D'Aquino (family) 42
d'Arieniello, Prince of 131
D'Avalos, Cesare, Marquis of Aragon 127
D'Avalos, Francesco 127
De Campo, Francesco 81
de Castro, Francisco 135
de Castro, Pedro Fernandez 135
De Dominicis, Antonio 42
De Felice, Ezio Bruno 188
de Forbin, Auguste 206
Dehnhardt, Federico 139
del Balzo (family) 244
del Balzo, Bertrando III 42
del Carretto, Ippolita 104
de Lione, Andrea 142
de Lione, Onofrio 142
della Rocca, Francesco 63
della Rocca, Prince 59
della Saponara, Count 68
della Torre, Giovanni Maria 183
del Po, Giacomo 81, 82, 131
de Maria, Francesco 131
De Martino, Aniello 127
De Mura, Francesco 76, 135, 142, 146, 148, 190, 244
de Nomé, François 23
de Pompeis, Alberto 240
de Ponte, Antonio 81
De Rossi, Giovan Giacomo 135, 142
de Sade, Donatien Alphonse François 97, 183
de' Sangro, Alessandro 101
de' Sangro, Antonio 104
de' Sangro di Mencaglia, Paolo 104
de' Sangro (family) 112, 116
de' Sangro, Gianfrancesco 94, 101, 104
de' Sangro, Marianna Duchess of Casacalenda 236
de' Sangro, Michele II 98, 101
de' Sangro, Paolo, Prince of Sansevero 94, 104, 109
de' Sangro, Placido, Count of Marsi 264
de' Sangro, Raimondo 94, 97, 101, 104, 112
de' Sangro, Vincenzo 104
Desiderio, Costantino 256
De Simone, Antonio 142

de Tommaso, Gaetano 240
de Vivo, Tommaso 142
de Zuñica, Juan, Count of Miranda 132
Diano, Giacinto 174, 256
di Capua, Bartolomeo, Prince of Riccia 71, 76
di Capua (family) 68, 71
di Mauro, Ernesto 288
Di Palma, Giovan Francesco 71, 81
di Resta, Isabella 15
di Sangro, Luzio 226
Dolce, Pietro 64
Dominici, Antonio 63, 135, 142
Donadio, Giovanni 68
Donatello 42
Doria, Gino 64
Doria, Giovan Carlo 250
Doria, Marcantonio 250
d'Orsi, Achille 139
Drummond Lord 266
Dumas, Alexandre 154
Dupérac, Étienne 16
Duranti, Pietro 142, 148
Durazzeschi 135

Egizio, Matteo 167
Eugenio di Savoia 119

Fanzago, Cosimo 59, 128, 157, 158, 236
Farnese, Elisabetta 176
Felice, Domenico 44
Ferdinand of Aragon, Count of 55
Ferdinand Bourbon 258
Ferdinand IV 136, 146, 183, 187, 199, 201
Fergola, Salvatore 31, 209
Ferrajolo, Angelo 44
Ferrante I 42
Ferrari, Francesco Saverio 282
Fici, Rosa of the Dukes of Amalfi 272
Fiengo, Giuseppe 236
Filangieri (family) 51
Filangieri, Gaetano, Prince of Satriano 46, 48
Filomarino della Rocca (family) 59, 63, 64
Finelli, Vitale 97
Firenze 10, 13, 14, 55
palazzo della Signoria 14
palazzo Strozzi 14
Fischetti, Alessandro 256
Fischetti, Fedele 230, 244, 256
Fisher, Giovanni Sigismondo 201
Fontana, Domenico 132, 135, 250
Francavilla, Princes of 187
Franceschi, Emilio 139
Francesco di Filippo da Settignano 44
Francesco di Giorgio Martini 71
Francesconi, Antonio 256, 298
Franchini, Michele 296
Fuga, Ferdinando 29, 90, 136, 142, 148, 180, 183, 199, 215, 216, 244, 250

Gaeta 89
Gaetani d'Aragona, Giulia 104
Gaetani dell'Aquila d'Aragona, Carlotta 104
Gaetani dell'Aquila d'Aragona, Cecilia 104
Galbiati, Giuseppe 42
Gamba, Crescenzo 199, 201, 234, 244
Gargiulo, Domenico (known as Micco Spadaro) 23
Garzilli, Duke of 131
Gauvadan, Francesco 136, 298
Gemito, Vincenzo 139
Genevois, Maria 298, 304
Genova 180
Genovese, Gaetano 135, 136, 139, 146, 148, 272, 276
Genovesi, Antonio 112
Gentileschi, Artemisia 142
Gerard, F. 206
Geri, Francesco 199
Gesuè, Carlo 136
Gigante, Giacinto 31
Gioffredo, Mario 226, 236, 240, 243, 250
Giordano, Giuseppe 266
Giordano, Luca 148, 190
Giordano, Tommaso 187
Giudice (family) 89
Giudice, Antonio, Prince of Cellamare and Duke of Giovinazzo 89, 90
Giuliano da Maiano 44, 71
Giustiniani, Michelangelo 226, 240
Goethe, Johann Wolfgang 28, 183
Gonzaga, Giulia 81
Graham, Elisa 101
Granet, François Maria 206
Grenier de la Croix, Charles 28
Gricc, Giuseppe 201
Gricc, Stefano 201
Grifeo, Benedetto, Prince of Partanna 258
Griffon, Giovanni Maria 256
Gualtieri 215
Guerra, Andrea 210, 215, 216
Guerra, Camillo 139
Guesdon, Alfred 31
Guidetti, Antonio 59
Gusman Carafa, Nicola 89
Guzman, Ramino 157

Hackert, Philipp 28
Herculaneum 23, 187, 192, 195, 201, 209
Herder, Johann Gottfried 28
Holbien, Hans the Younger 26
Houel, Jean 28
Huraut, Giulio 298, 303, 304

Il Cairo 10
Imperiali, Michele 93
Ippodamo di Mileto 12

Jerace, Francesco 139
Joanna of Anjou 52
Joli, Antonio 28, 148
Juvarra, Filippo 216

Labrot, Gérard 16, 24, 25
Lacis, Asja 10
Ladislao of Durazzo 38, 52, 56, 60
Lafréry, Antonio 16, 246
Laperuta, Leopoldo 136
Lazzari, Dionisio 149
Lazzari, Giacomo 101
Lecomte, Étienne Cherubin 202
Ledoux, Claude-Nicolas 30
Lemasle, Louis Nicolas 209
Le Nôtre, André 199
Liani, Felice 146
Limatola (family) 116
Lingelbach, Johannes 28
Lipsia 59
Loffredo, Gerolama 104
London 10, 28
Hampton Court 195
Louis of Aragon 52
Louis XIV 199
Lusieri, Giovan Battista 28

Maddaloni, Duke of 250
Madrid 150
el Escorial 195
Maffei, Giovan Battista 76
Magri, Gaetano 234, 244
Magri, Giuseppe 234, 244
Maldarelli, Federico 187
Maldarelli, Gennaro 148
Mangone, Fabio 266
Manlio, Ferdinando 84, 93, 132
Manni, Giovan Battista 89, 90
Manzi (family) 158
Marchese, Luigi 30
Maria Amalia of Saxony 135, 142, 187
Maria Cristina Bourbon 146
Marie Caroline of Austria 136, 258
Marigliano (family) 76
Marigliano, Saverio 68
Marsiglia 10, 44
Martin, P.E. 206
Martorelli, Luisa 201, 202
Marziale 41
Masaccio 190
Masaniello 23, 63, 127, 128, 157
Massa, Giuseppe 76
Matera 52
Maurizio Emanuele di Lorena, Prince of Elboeuf 195, 220
Medina Las Torres, Duke of 150, 154, 157
Medinacoeli, Duke of 89
Medrano, Giovanni Antonio 179, 195, 199
Mencaglia, Giulio 101
Mengs, Anton Raphael 244
Meyer 28
Micco Spadaro (see Domenico Gargiulo)
Migliaccio, Giuseppe 264
Migliaccio, Lucia Duchess of Floridia 258, 264
Migliaccio, Luigi 264
Migliaccio, Marianna 261, 264
Milano 30, 55, 290
Milano, Laudonia 104
Milizia, Francesco 278
Miranda, Duke of 131
Mirelli, Carlo, Marquis of Teora 158
Mirelli, Gaetana Marches of Teora 104
Molajoli, Bruno 188
Monaco, Nymphenburg 195
Moncada di Paternò, Agata, Princess of Satriano 51
Monsù Desiderio 23
Montesquieu, Charles de Secondat 135
Monticelli, Teodoro 41
Morano, Antonio 101
Morelli, Domenico 187
Mormando (Giovanni Donadio) 63, 71, 116
Moscati, Nicola 167
Muller, Peter 148
Murat, Carolina 206
Murat, Gioacchino 59, 149, 187, 201, 206

Naples
ALBERGO DEI POVERI 210-219, 29
Biblioteca nazionale Vittorio Emanuele III 136
borgo Loreto 216
bell tower della chiesa di Santa Chiara 63
Capodichino 31
Capodimonte 179
Capodimonte Hill 179
Capuana district 13
Castel Capuano 84
Castel dell'Ovo 89
CASTELLO ASELMEYER 306-314
Castel Nuovo 13, 36, 41, 42, 132
Castel san Martino 10
Castel Sant'Elmo 17, 23, 89
castello del Carmine 216
cemetery Nuovo 30
Chiaia 17, 87
Churches
Monteoliveto 127
San Demetrio 81
San Domenico Maggiore 42
San Francesco di Paola 30, 136
Santa Brigida 294
Santa Maria della Rotonda 236, 240
Santa Maria della Stella 71
Stanta Maria del Pianto 148
Santi Severino e Sossio 71
cloister of Santa Chiara 41
corso Umberto 36
corso Vittorio Emanuele 304, 306, 314
Court della Vicaria Vecchia 56
depositi dei Granili 29, 216
Foro Murat 15
giardino Italia 136
gradinata di Santa Barbara 41
GRAND EDEN HOTEL 298-305
isolotto della Gayola 311
largo dello Spirito Santo 124, 246, 250, 252
largo di Palazzo 15, 135, 136
largo San Demetrio 38
Mergellina 20, 150, 154
molo San Vincenzo 20
monastery of Gerolamini 37
monastery of San Severo Maggiore 46
Montagna district 13
monte Echia 17, 20, 31
monte Palatino 14
Montesanto 17
Mortelle Hill 93
museums
Archeologico nazionale 187, 188
Artistico industriale 51
Civico Gaetano Filangieri 46, 51
delle carrozze 276
Diego Aragona Pignatelli Cortes 276
Nazionale della ceramica duca di Martina 264
Nazionale di San Martino 260, 264
Nido district 13, 71
ospizio di San Gennaro dei Poveri 210
Palaces
Acquaviva d'Atri 25, 36, 71
Balzorano 298, 304
Bisignano (see Filomarino)
Bonifacio 38
Brancaccio (see Filomarino)
Capone 288, 394
Caracciolo d'Oppido 67
CARAFA 38-43, 71
Carafa della Spina 36, 71
Carafa di Maddaloni 8, 15
Carafa di Montorio 71
Caramanico 199, 201
CASACALENDA 236-245, 226, 230
CASSAMASSINA 78-83, 25, 36, 37
CELLAMARE 84-93
CORIGLIANO 116-123, 36, 71
CUOMO 44-51, 41
D'ANGOLO DELLA GALLERIA UMBERTO I 288-297
D'ANGRI 246-257, 15, 37
d'Avalos 127
dei Regi Studi 187, 188
dell'abate di San Giovanni Maggiore 78
DELLO SPAGNUOLO 162-167, 170
del Panomita 71
di Capua (see Marigliano)
DONN'ANNA 150-161, 8, 20, 29
Filangieri di Arianello 36
FILOMARINO 60-67, 36, 52, 56, 81
Gravina 67
MADDALONI 124-131, 25, 90, 252, 256
MARIGLIANO 68-77, 15
Mascabruno 195, 209
Melofioccolo 81
of the Marquis of Vasto 93
of Queen Joanna 150, 154
Orsini di Gravina 15, 81
PENNE 38-43, 8, 15
PETRUCCI 38-43, 36
REALE 132-149, 15, 37, 89, 201
REALE DI CAPOODIMONTE 176-191, 29, 136, 192, 195, 234, 244
Reale Vecchio 84, 124
RUFFO DELLA SCALETTA 278-287
SANFELICE 162-167
Sanfelice ai Vergini 36
San Marco 52
Sanseverino (now Church of the Gesù) 15, 36, 81
SANSEVERO 94-115
SERRA DI CASSANO 168-175, 282
Spinelli di Tarsia 8, 25, 37
VENICE 52-59, 36, 60, 63, 64
palazzina Rotschild 272
parco Grifeo 306
Piazzas
Mercato 128
Plebiscito 15, 132, 136, 139, 142
San Domenico Maggiore 36, 42, 116, 226, 236, 240, 243
San Ferdinando 135
San Giovanni Maggiore 78
Santa Caterina (now piazza dei Martiri) 258
Trieste and Trento 136
Pizzofalcone 17, 168, 282
ponte della Maddalena 23
Portanuova district 13
porticato dell'Incoronata 41
Porto district 13
Posillipo 20, 31, 150, 157, 158, 311
Riviera di Chiaia 30, 37, 266, 272, 278, 298
Santa Lucia 31
slargo di Monteoliveto 15, 17
Spirito Santo 127
strada di Santa Maria di Loreto 216
teatro Mercadante 294
teatro San Carlino 288
teatro San Carlo 30, 132, 136, 260, 294
Università degli studi Federico II 81, 209
Vasto 31
Vesuvius 20, 23, 26, 29, 192, 196, 199, 226
vie
Arenaccia 216
Atri 36
Banchi Nuovi 78
Benedetto Croce 36, 52, 59
Chiatamone 314
dei Mille 31, 298
del Campo 216, 219
del Carogioiello (see via Tommaso Senise)
del parco Margherita 31, 298, 304
del Sole 122
Domenico Capitelli 128
Duomo 31, 46, 48
Egiziaca 168
Filangieri 31, 298
Foria 36
Lucrezia d'Alagno 48
Maddaloni 127, 128, 131
Marina 36
Mezzocannone 31, 236, 240, 244
Monte di Dio 168
Monteoliveto 250
Municipo (now via Verdi) 288
Nilo 36, 250
Posillipo 160
San Biagio dei Librai 71
San Gregorio Armento 68
San Sebastiano 56
Santa Brigida 288
Santa Lucia 314
Sant'Anna dei Lombardi 127, 246
Toledo 37, 124, 127, 131, 246 250, 252, 256
Tomasso Senise 127, 128, 131, 256
Vittoria Colonna 298
Vicaria 24
vicolo di Santa Barbara 41
vicolo Pallonetto a Santa Chiara 236
vico San Geronimo 78
ville
ACTON PIGNATELLI 266-277, 30, 37
Belvedere 37, 157
Bonifacio 157
CAMPOLIETO 220-235
Doria D'Angri 30
EBE 306-314
FLORIDIANA 258-265, 30
La Favorita 187
Lucia 30, 260
Reale 30
villino Colonna Pignatelli 298
Vomero 31, 37, 258
Nauclerio, Giovanni Battista 90
Niccolini, Antonio 136, 187, 260, 266
Nigrone, Antonio 81

Olivares, Duke of 150
Onelli, Fortunato 104
Orsini di Gravina (family) 81
Orsini, Lelio 81
Orsini, Pietro, Prince of Solofra 81
Ortese, Anna Maria 29
Ottaiano, Prince of 131

Pacecco Carafa, Diomede Marzio 131
Paisiello,Giovanni 142
Palena, Count of 195, 199
Palermo 183, 187
palazzo reale 142
Paliotti, Vincenzo 276
Pane, Roberto 20, 24, 36, 38, 41, 64, 67, 71, 216
Papworth, Edgard 31
Paris 10, 28, 101
place de l'Etoile 31
Parma 179
Parmigianino 190
Passero 136
Patturelli, Giovanni 201
Pedro Alvarez da Toledo 16, 17, 20, 124, 132, 135
Penne (family) 41
Penne, Antonio 38, 41
Penne, Luca 41
Penne, Onofrio 41
Perrotta 42
Persico, Paolo 101, 104
Petrella, Marquis of 20
Petrucci, Antonello 42
Phillip III 132
Phillip IV 150
Phillip Bourbon 89, 176
Phillip of Aragon 124, 132
Piacenza 179
Picchiatti, Bartolomeo 59, 97, 167
Picchiatti, Francesco Antonio 89, 135
Pietroburgo 30
Pignatelli (family) 276
Pignatelli, Camillo, Duke of Monteleone 127
Pimentel d'Errera, Juan Alfonso 135
Pius IV, Pope 202
Pompei 23, 187, 192, 209, 220
Portici 154, 195, 201, 220
REGGIA 192-209, 29, 136, 187, 192, 220
Porzio, Michelangelo 240
Preti, Matthia 148, 174
priore della Roccella 128
Pugliano 199

Quierolo, Francesco 101, 104

Ranucci, Bartolomeo 120
Renato d'Angiò 55
Resina (now Heraculaneum) 187, 195, 220
Restile, Luigi 201
Re, Vincenzo 142, 199, 201
Ribera, Jusepe de 190
Riccardo di Albignano 44
Ripa, Cesare 122
Robert of Anjou 41
Rocca (family) 41
Rocco, Emanuele 288, 294, 296
Rocco, Gregorio Maria 215
Rome 10, 13, 14, 28, 127, 128, 132, 135, 183, 244
church of San Francesco 195
church of Sant'Eustachio 195
palazzo Farnese 14, 187, 278
palazzo Venezia 48
Roomer, Gaspare 127
Rosa, Salvator 23
Rossi Romano, Gaetano 294
Rotili, Mario 71
Rotolo, Hellen 42
Rotschild, Carlo von 272
Ruiz de Castro, Fernandez, Count of Lemos 132, 135
Russo, Francesco Maria 101
Ruta, Clemente 201

Sacco, Annibale 187, 188
Saliceti, Angelica 258
Saliceti, Caterina 258
Saliceti, Cristoforo 258, 260
Salluzzo, Agostino, Duke of Corigliano 116, 119
San Giorgio a Cremano 195
San Giovanni a Carbonara 167
San Giovanni a Teduccio 195, 220
San Giuliano, Marquis of 127
Sanchez, Alfonso, Marquis of Grottola 78
Sanfelice, Ferdinando 67, 81, 136, 162, 167, 168, 170, 180, 195, 282
Sanfelice, Giovanni 90
Sanfelice, Guglielmo 25
Sanmartino, Giuseppe 97, 109, 167
Sanseverino (family) 52
Sanseverino di Bisignano (family) 63
Sanseverino di Bisignano, Bernardino 63
Sanseverino, Amerigo conte di Capaccio 55
Santafede, Fabrizio 174
Santobuono, Prince of 195
Saponieri 298
Sasso, Camillo 278, 286
Savoia (family) 187
Scaniglia 216
Scannapieco (family) 41
Scannapieco, Aloise 41
Scannasorice, Francesco 46
Schiantarelli, Pompeo 36
Sciacca, Steripinto 38
Serao, Matile 24
Serra, Gennaro 168
Simone Martini 190
Sinosa, Nicola 244
Sisto V, Pope 132, 135
Solari, Tommaso 139
Solferino, Gerardo 97
Solimena, Francesco 167, 190, 256
Soufflot, Jacques-Germaine 216
Spagna 135, 183, 201
Spinosa, Nicola 174, 230
Stanzione, Massimo 142
Starace, Girolamo 256
Stopendaal, Bastiaen 17
Strabone 11
Summonte 71

Tanucci, Bernardo 116, 183
Teano 42
Thuret 149
Tiarini, Alessandro 174
Tijstheuschi, Mattia 81
Tolfa, Isabella 104
Tomeo, Basso 154
Torella, Marquis of 127
Torre del Greco 220
Traversi, Gaspare 190
Trevisan, Angelo 298
Turner, William 28

Vaccaro, Andrea 148
Vaccaro, Domenico Antonio 25, 37, 135, 142
Valente, Pietro 266, 269
Valenti Gonzaga, cardinale 215
Van Essen, Jan 23
Vanvitelli, Carlo 250
Vanvitelli, Luigi 29, 136, 142, 196, 199, 216, 226, 230, 234, 240, 243, 244, 252, 253
Vasari, Giorgio 78, 190
Vecellio, Tiziano 190
Venditti, Arnaldo 195, 278
Venice 52, 55
palazzo Ducale 14
Venuti, Domenico 187
Versailles 195, 199
Vico, Giambattista 64
Vittorio Emanuele III 188
Viva, Angelo 142
Volaire, Pierre-Jacques 28

Wijck, Thomas 26
Winckelmann, Johann Joachim 183
Wutzky, Michael 28

Young, Lamont 306, 311, 314

Ziattino di Benozzis da Settignano 44
Zoccoli, Carlo 240

First Printing
December 1999
EBS - Editoriale Bortolazzi STEI
San Giovanni Lupatoto (VR) - Italy
E-mail: ebs@ebs-bortolazzi.com